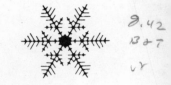

# TEACH YOUR CHILD TO SKI

# TEACH YOUR CHILD TO SKI

## BARBARA ANN COCHRAN
### AND
## LINDY COCHRAN KELLEY
### with Craig A. Altschul

THE STEPHEN GREENE PRESS
PELHAM BOOKS

**THE STEPHEN GREENE PRESS/PELHAM BOOKS**

Published by the Penguin Group
Viking Penguin, a division of Penguin Books USA Inc.,
    40 West 23rd Street, New York, New York 10010, U.S.A.
Penguin Books Ltd., 27 Wrights Lane, London W8 5TZ, England
Penguin Books Australia Ltd, Ringwood, Victoria, Australia
Penguin Books Canada Ltd, 2801 John Street,
    Markham, Ontario, Canada L3R 1B4
Penguin Books (N.Z.) Ltd, 182-190 Wairau Road, Auckland 10, New Zealand

Penguin Books Ltd, Registered Offices: Harmondsworth, Middlesex, England

First published in 1989 by The Stephen Green Press/Pelham Books

Distributed by Viking Penguin, a division of Penguin Books USA Inc.

10  9  8  7  6  5  4  3  2  1

Photographs by Douglas Aja

**Library of Congress Cataloging-in-Publication Data**
Cochran, Barbara.
    Teach your child to ski / by Barbara Cochran and Lindy Cochran
Kelley with Craig A. Altschul.
        p.        cm.
    "Pelham books."
    ISBN 0-8289-0717-X
    1. Skiing for children—Study and teaching. I. Kelley, Lindy
Cochran. II. Altschul, Craig A. III. Title
GV854.32.C58        1989
796.93083'3—dc19                                            89-7556
                                                                 CIP

Printed in the United States of America
Designed by Michael Michaud
Set in Garamond and Futura by CopyRight, Bedford, MA
Produced by Unicorn Production Services, Inc.

## DEDICATION

We would like to dedicate this book
to our parents, Mickey and Ginny Cochran,
who started it all.

# CONTENTS

## ACKNOWLEDGEMENTS

Our sincere thanks to all those people
who made this book possible, especially to:
Everyone at Stephen Greene Press
for their guidance and support;
Craig Altschul for his creative talents;
Tommy, Jimmy, Amy, Jessica, Timmy,
Roger, Douglas, Preston, and Tell
for their patience in being our guinea pigs;
a special thanks to Doug Aja for his versatility,
creativity, and patience while taking the photographs;
the Chuck Perkins family at the Alpine Shop,
who were very generous with their expertise and facilities;
Rossignol Ski Company, Marker U.S.A., and Shelburne
Industries, who supplied equipment for the photos;
C B Sports and Peter Dodge,
who supplied clothing for the photos;
And a special thanks to all those children we have taught,
who in turn have taught us so much.

# SKIING'S FIRST FAMILY: THE COCHRANS
## by Craig A. Altschul

These are heady days in the ski industry. Downhill skiing has become a worldwide, multibillion-dollar business. Giant international conglomerates operate dozens of ski areas. Executives in distant boardrooms pore over stacks of green-lined financial projections, listening to marketing experts outline ad campaigns and talk about "the demographics of the ski area user target population." Skiing, in other words, is big time.

On the slopes much has changed, too. Zippy gondolas carry you to the top of the mountain in moments. Mid-mountain restaurants serve gourmet meals. Shops carry the latest in brilliant fashions and high-tech ski equipment. Ski instructors sweep your kids off to a "learning center" for instruction, and woe betide you if you even *think* of teaching your kids to ski by yourself.

Sometimes that's great. The big changes in the ski industry have increased many skiers' enjoyment. Sometimes, though, it's all a bit too much: too much speed, too much flash, too much money.

Remember when it wasn't like this? Remember when your parents first strapped a pair of boards on your feet and set you sliding downhill at a simple, small, unhurried slope?

Well, the Cochran family remembers. And at the Cochran Family Ski Area in northern Vermont, two parents who loved skiing produced the most awesome family of ski racers in American history: Marilyn, Barbara Ann, Bobby, and Lindy Cochran.

The Cochrans' operation proves that the mom-and-pop ski area isn't an endangered species. Ginny (Mom) runs the snack bar and the ski school. Mickey (Dad) runs the ski area. Lindy and Barbara Ann help parents teach their kids how to ski on little Cochran Hill, where a chair lift wouldn't dare to disturb the landscape; where one of the last of the Mitey Mite lifts reigns supreme.

Who are these people and why do they own such a special place in the hearts of those who have followed ski racing over the years? And why should we listen to their ideas about teaching kids to ski?

## ONE WORD APPLIES: DOMINATION

Never in American history has one family so totally dominated the sport of ski racing—or any other sport—as did the Cochrans in the 1970s.

The crowning achievement, of course, came at the Winter Olympic Games at Sapporo, Japan, when Barbara Ann won the Gold Medal in the slalom. Bob was the top American finisher in the downhill in eighth place, and had he not locked a tip in the second run of the slalom he might have won it.

Marilyn raced for the United States in the downhill, slalom, and the giant slalom. Lindy went on to the Innsbruck Olympics in 1976 and finished sixth in the slalom and twelfth in the giant slalom—in both cases, the top American finisher.

"I was confident I had the ability to win," says Barbara Ann, speaking of Sapporo. "I wasn't concerned with how anyone else was doing. I went by the family philosophy that if we concentrated on our skills, the results would take care of themselves." She is currently organizing her own business showing parents how to teach their children to ski.

At the 1970 International Ski Federation (FIS) World Championships (the "Skiing Olympics"), Barbara Ann won the silver medal in slalom and Marilyn took the bronze medal for the combined competition.

Between the years 1972 and 1978, all members of the family had competed in one or more olympiad, representing the United States Ski Team, and Mickey had served a year as coach of the team.

The Cochran family so dominated the action at the United States Alpine Championships each year that they can count at least fifteen total national titles in their heyday. Bobby wore six consecutive national crowns himself. Just to add insult to injury (hardly a phrase ski racers would like me to use), Marilyn competed in the 1971 French National Championships the first time an American was allowed to do so, and won the slalom, giant slalom, and combined titles and was third in the downhill.

They amassed seven World Cup wins, ten second-place finishes, and five thirds. Their top-ten finishes were everyday events.

Want more? Marilyn won the 1969 overall World Cup giant slalom crown her sophomore year on the circuit, and Barbara Ann was second in the overall slalom campaign and third in giant slalom in 1970. Bobby remains the only American male skier to finish in the top three in a World Cup slalom, giant slalom, and downhill in a single season.

Credentials? All four Cochran kids were ranked in the world's top seed in *at least* two events: Bobby and Marilyn in slalom, giant slalom, and downhill; Barbara Ann and Lindy in both slalom and giant slalom. That alone is an incredible, never-before—never-after—feat.

One of the Cochrans was always in the hunt for a medal or a title or a win, seldom finishing out of striking distance.

Before hanging up the competition skis, Bobby took on the World Professional Ski Tour for a few years, finishing third overall in 1976.

## GLITZ AND GLAMOUR? NO WAY

Unlike racers who would come along later, the Cochrans retired before their time—at least before the time when companies paid lucrative endorsements that kept racers' visibility high for years after the racing ended.

But that's not the Cochran family style. Glitz and glamour give way to family, friends, and kids. The family comes first; always has, always will.

The only high-speed anything at the Cochran Family Ski Area these days is the hundreds of local kids who bash through the gates after school and on weekends. Marketing is a black-and-white brochure from the local printery. Word-of-mouth advertising brings out the kids and parents.

The ski school is Cochran certified, and with this family's trophy display, does it need any stamp of approval?

There are (at last count) seven Cochrans in the newest generation. All were taught by their respective parents at the Cochran Family Ski Area.

By now you may be thinking: "Of course the Cochrans can teach *their* kids to ski; they're among the best skiers in the world."

True. The Cochrans are world-class skiers and ski racers. That's as clear as the echoes from victory stands of old.

The fact is, the Cochran method works. There are hundreds upon hundreds of kids (now grown-ups or on their way toward that inevitable plateau) who have been taught to ski by their parents using the Cochran concept as a base.

You can do it, too.

What follows in this book are successful techniques proven and distilled for you by Barbara Ann and Lindy. They prove their theories work every weekend.

The premise is that if you have plenty of patience and you are a reasonably good skier, you can teach your kids to ski all by yourself. And, you can do it at Aspen or Vail, Mammoth or Bear Mountain, Mount Cranmore or Camelback.

If you're really lucky, and you live close enough to the Cochrans' backyard, you can do it right there, after, of course, you master riding the Mitey Mite.

Barbara Ann and Lindy think you can teach your children to ski. There will be those who disagree, but there are those who disagree with all simple theories. Tom, Jimmy, Amy, Jessica, Roger, Douglas, and Timmy Cochran will ski the pants off those naysayers.

Your kids can, too.

# TEACH YOUR CHILD TO SKI

# O N E
# YOU CAN DO IT

Let's get right to it.

Any child who can walk can learn to ski.

Whether you happen to be the parent of a tot or of an older child, *you* can teach your own Jimmy or Jessica to ski if you follow the Cochran method.

You will begin to see your son or daughter in a different light, and the rewards will come to both of you each time a new accomplishment comes along, no matter how trivial it may seem.

Skiing can truly be a family affair and is one of only a handful of sports where that honestly can be said. What else is there: swimming, skating, hiking? Maybe, but skiing *truly* works for families— if families *truly* work at skiing together.

We have taught kids to ski for over twenty-five years, and this book has been designed to share our methods—our successes and experiences—with you. Our own parents taught us to ski when we were tots. Now, as we have children, we are teaching them to ski.

When the two-, three-, and five-year-old Cochrans head down the hill, people turn their heads to watch. ''Skiing is in their genes,'' they muse. Maybe, maybe not.

The Cochran family kids *are* expert skiers. All of us: Marilyn, Barbara Ann, Lindy, and Bobby. We fine-tuned our skills to compete all over the world for the United States Ski Team. We've run gates in Vermont, Colorado, Utah, and California, Switzerland and Austria, Italy and Japan—and probably everywhere else in the world where racing gates have ever been set. We've competed in junior championships, World Cup races, World Alpine Ski Championships, and the ultimate—the Winter Olympic Games.

We're confident in our abilities, and that confidence has allowed us to experiment in techniques. With our children to practice with, it's made it fun, too.

The skiing Cochrans in 1971. From left, Ginny, Lindy, Mickey, Barbara Ann, Marilyn, and Bobby.

The four of us are separated by three and one-half years. We grew up as friends and playmates, and you can be sure that if there is anything one of us did, the others weren't far behind.

We were dominating races in northern Vermont by the time we were getting ready for junior high school. Since we were winning so much, people began to wonder if our parents were pushing us too hard or, worse, punishing us when we didn't win.

Actually, the *opposite* was the case.

We won and we skied so much and so well because there *wasn't any pressure* on us. Mom and Dad gave us direction, but they never pushed us.

Simply put, we did so well because of their philosophy of *never* putting pressure on us.

We were encouraged to believe in ourselves. We never thought that something was impossible. Sure, it might be difficult, but we'd always give it a try. And, though it seems a bit trite to put in these terms, their guideline was always, "If at first you don't succeed, try, try again."

Nobody worried about whether we won or not; we just wanted to compete against the best skiers around. We were instilled with the idea that we could learn from better competitors, so we strove to get to those levels.

"If at first you don't succeed, try, try again."

## THE BEST YOU CAN BE

Barbara Ann remembers bringing home her third grade report card, when she had received her first C mark. She was afraid to show it to Mom. When Mom asked if it really was the best she could do and Barbara Ann said, Yes, it was, Mom said something none of us has ever forgotten. "I don't care if you get all Fs on your report card, as long as it's the best you can do."

Mom and Dad never said, "We want you to win this race." They helped us make sure we memorized the course, knew our line coming through the gates, understood we knew when we could set up and where we needed to run straight. They concentrated on the skills they wanted us to learn, not on the final results.

What they were doing was helping us develop a game plan.

We never worried about the turns we did poorly; we concentrated on the one turn we did so well. There's a wonderful Vince Lombardi quote where he said, "We never lost a game; we just ran out of time." Somehow, it applies.

Over the years, we have taught hundreds of people to ski, from tiny tots to teenagers to adults. We have developed our own convictions, philosophies, and programs that work.

Think about your own family or families with whom you ski: the younger kids are either left home with grandma or warehoused in the day-care center at the ski area while you—mom and dad— spend a day on the slopes enjoying yourselves.

We don't think there is any need for that. None at all.

Many ski schools aren't interested in taking tots into their programs for a variety of reasons.

And, the truth is, lots of those reasons are valid.

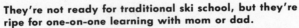

**They're not ready for traditional ski school, but they're ripe for one-on-one learning with mom or dad.**

## LEARNING FROM MOM OR DAD

Children at this age (three to five) are not ready to learn in a traditional ski school class. But, they are certainly ready to learn something new on a one-on-one basis with mom or dad.

There are many differences between three-, four-, and five-year-olds. A three-year-old might only be able to walk a few steps on skis, while a five-year-old enjoys clomping around.

We have learned how to overcome the obstacles in our Ski Tots Program because we've encouraged parents to be with their kids one-on-one.

Carving is a term from ski racing that we feel is very important for control. It shows the kids that skis can turn for them and there's no need to push the skis around. We'll refer often to the technique of carving in this book.

Today's ski equipment is far better than that on which our family learned to ski. It's better made, faster, and easier to ski on. But, it can lead to out-of-control skiers.

By emphasizing carving, we have emphasized control right from the very beginning.

Every child will, of course, need to learn the very same basic skills, but ages dictate lengths of attention spans and each youngster is different in his or her ability to learn.

Tots are almost helpless and they need individual, one-on-one instruction. They have an extremely short attention span and they take longer to learn a skill. To be successful, the instruction needs to be fun, imaginative, and certainly safe.

With more physically mature youngsters, ages six to ten, there's a growing independent spirit. These kids improve quickly, adapt to skills in a hurry, and love to play skill-oriented games. They are marvelous imitators and will listen to verbal instructions, as long as they are kept brief and clear.

## TOTS AND OLDER CHILDREN

We've divided our book into sections dealing with tots and older children.

We do our best to explain basic skills, and you may find that we're providing a tip or two for your own skiing along the way.

Sometimes we'll suggest a game to play where you can encourage skill development while having fun together.

Children, ages six to ten, learn well because they are wonderful imitators.

And be sure and use the checklists at the end of each chapter for a quick review before you head out on the hill.

Set yourself up for success by eliminating pressures. Provide the opportunity to learn to ski, but don't push. Give direction, but listen, too.

Believe that Timmy can and will succeed at skiing, and let him know you are sure he can learn that specific skill. Let him know it's OK to fall or to make a mistake. The important thing to get across is that he should keep trying.

Keep your expectations in check.

Perhaps 99 percent of the time, Timmy won't accomplish the skill; then, suddenly, he will. His personal best may not be what you expect. "Is that the best you can do?" you'll ask.

"You can do better than that!" is a phrase to toss into the snowbank. Don't ever say it.

Everyone—tots to older kids to you personally—has good days and bad days on skis or in learning any skill. Don't compare good and bad days and don't compare Timmy to Tom. Concentrate on that personal best. Timmy only has control over himself; he has no control whatsoever on how Tom is learning.

When Timmy finds himself out of control (and he will), you can yell "turn, turn, turn" all day long and it won't help. Timmy would turn if he could, because the last thing in the world he wants is to be out of control.

**The important thing is to keep trying!**

When things come back to normal, advise Timmy to push his ski tails out into a V, push the right ski out more than the left, and lean to the right. Again, concentrate on the skills, not the results.

Praise is important and it works wonders. But keep it sincere, not offering praise for something he didn't do.

"Hey, Timmy," you'll say. "You walked around that circle without slipping backward once! Good for you!"

## PRAISE IS THE REWARD

Every achievement counts; nothing is too minimal to mention. The reward for triumph is praise. It works on Cochran Hill and it works on the way to the Olympic victory stand.

We wrote this book because family values are very important to us.

And, just for the record, Mom and Dad weren't World Cup skiers. They were just Mom and Dad.

They didn't push us. They encouraged us to do our best.

That's just what you can do for your own Timmy, Tom, and Jessica.

# SKIING IS A FAMILY SPORT

Magic is a funny word; it describes so much. When we were growing up, winter was our magic time. It still is today.

We grew up skiing. We got up early on Saturday and Sunday mornings and did our chores and packed lunches. By a little after 7:00 A.M., we were all crammed into the station wagon, surrounded by skis, boots, and poles.

Our weekend adventures began when we arrived at the ski area. These were wonderful times for our family; we achieved a sense of togetherness that would probably have been impossible in any other sport. Perhaps, just as important, those times created memories that will last a lifetime.

Our parents loved skiing. And teaching us to ski meant a great deal to them. They knew what we now know: learning to ski provides a person—no matter how old—with a tremendous sense of accomplishment. Risking a cliché or two, the sport is healthy, exciting, and challenging.

Remember when you were a beginning skier? Of course you do. You stood on the top of a little hill that looked like the Matterhorn. You probably felt the same way you'd feel if you were sitting in a car on top of a hill without a steering wheel or brakes. How do you turn? How do you stop? Who's running this show, anyway, you or the skis? It can be frightening at first.

Yet, with some patience and the right attitude, you discovered the steering wheel that had been there all along. You learned how to work the brakes. At each point along the way you felt a sense of excitement, of exhilaration, of accomplishment.

The entire family—at any age and ability level along the scale—can enjoy skiing at the same place at the same time.

When we were very young, ranging from one to four years old, Mom and Dad bought a family pass at Mount Ascutney Ski Area in Brownsville, Vermont.

Skiing brought us a sense of togetherness. That's Bobby, age six; Lindy, age four; and Barbara Ann, age seven, in a photo taken in 1958.

Accomplishment is the important word. Here is Lindy entering her first Lollipop race in 1957 at Mount Ascutney, Vermont.

Dad was coaching the Windsor High School ski team, and they trained on the Mount Ascutney practice slope. Mom skied on the expert trails. We'd play and ski with our friends on the beginner hill.

Lindy and her friend, "Snowball" Ely, could be found building snowmen in front of the lodge. But we never failed to all take a few runs together and then to share our adventures when the skiing had ended. We had a common bond—a six-letter word called skiing.

Building snowmen is always great adventure, and here's Lindy at age four with the start of a new creation.

## IT'S "WARM" OUTSIDE

It's always been interesting to us how parents bundle their children up and try *not* to let them stay outdoors too long to play.

Yet, in skiing, we're encouraging the kids to be outside during the winter months for five to seven hours at a time. We've discovered that kids don't need pampering when they're having fun. Most can be outside and active on skis for much of the day without going inside.

As children we were so anxious to get on the mountain that when we were a bit older and skiing at Smuggler's Notch, we'd have our boots on and buckled before the car had stopped in the parking lot. We'd be the first skiers up the hill when the lift cranked up at 8:00 A.M. We learned to time our runs just right, so we'd be on the last ride up the lift a second or two before 4:00 P.M.

When we finally had no choice but to go in, we'd rummage around for lunch. Oh, we know the nutritionists out there will scream, but when kids love to do something that's healthy and fun, let them do it. If they get hungry or cold, they'll stop and come in on their own.

Skiing isn't a sport that ends when the bell hits twenty-five or thirty. It's a lifetime sport that, once learned, becomes instinctive and never forgotten. Unlike so many other sports, you can enjoy skiing when you are fifty, sixty, seventy, and even eighty.

Some of our friends—now with kids of their own—haven't skied in fifteen years. They were afraid they had forgotten how to do it. Do you forget how to ride a bike? No. Because of the rapid-fire improvement in ski equipment, people who have been off the slopes for a while generally find the return much, much easier and more enjoyable than they remember it.

**Skiing is a sport for all ages, as this group of three generations of skiers proves.**

## A HEALTHY, FUN SPORT

Mom says she wanted us involved in skiing because it is such a healthy sport; perhaps, she laughs, it's because she saw it as a much better alternative than watching Saturday morning cartoon shows on television. Skiing meant her kids were exercising in the fresh mountain air, developing hearty appetites, playing with friends, and wearing themselves out so they slept like logs at night.

Dad saw skiing as a family sport, and he really spent time coaching us in ski racing because he saw it as a way of imparting some of life's lessons in a way we would be sure to learn.

His philosophy is that you have to work hard, and the more valuable something is to you, the harder it is to attain. No, Dad never dreamed that any — let alone all — of his children would be in the Olympics, but he instilled in us that if we wanted to do well in ski racing, we'd have to practice, practice, practice.

At this point, the family moved to South Burlington, Vermont, and we spent every weekend at Smuggler's Notch. After a few years of suburban living, we moved twelve miles east to a house with 100 acres.

You guessed it. Because weekend skiing wasn't enough for us, Dad built a rope tow up the backyard slope so we could train during the week, too.

That was the start of the Cochran Family Ski Area and is an example of how a family can learn to ski together and to grow up loving a sport. We did. You can, too, even if you don't happen to have a rope tow in your backyard.

We suppose there are some family experiences that are better enjoyed without the tots, but we'll argue that skiing is not one of those experiences.

The absolute best time to learn to ski is between the ages of three to five.

Beginners fall — it's part of learning to ski — but when you're little, it's not as far to fall. A tot is limber — much more so than an adult — and it's easier to get up again. They don't have our inherent, built-in fears, and they take to skiing much more naturally.

Skiing gives three- to five-year-olds an enormous sense of pride and accomplishment — independence, too. It gives us, as parents, a wonderful sense of pride. If you're like every other parent, you'll end up boasting to your friends about the days you spent cruising down the ski area trails, with Amy right behind.

There will come the day, too, as the great ski filmmaker Warren Miller loves to remind us, that Amy will pass you — forever.

One afternoon, when we were all on the U.S. Ski Team, we got a lesson in children's determination. We had taken a break from skiing gates to ski some runs with friends. With us was a five-year-old named Chuckie Buxton. We skied slowly with the group for a few runs but then decided to meet the others at the bottom and do an all-out free-skiing run to get our energy levels back up.

We blasted out, as we usually did, but we constantly heard some swishing sounds behind us. When we got to the bottom we were astounded. Guess who was right there with us? Yes, Chuckie Buxton.

OK, so not all five-year-olds are ready to keep up with the U.S. Ski Team, but it is possible to enjoy a run thoroughly with an accomplished ski tot.

## LOTS OF WAYS TO TEACH KIDS

There are lots of ways to teach your own children to ski, and we could spend plenty of pages giving you our opinions of which work and which don't.

There's the old-fashioned way, for example, of tossing the kid into the water and hoping he can swim. You know what we mean. Hike up the hill, point the skis down, and hope he gets there without getting hurt. Don't do it.

Some parents even fall for well-meaning friends (of all ages) saying, "Don't worry, we'll show them how to ski." They'll never go again. Don't do it this way, either.

Enough don'ts.

You could certainly outfit your son, Roger, pack him up and take him to the ski area, sign him up for lessons at the ski school desk, and hope there's the right chemistry between instructor, student, and classmates.

This is certainly an acceptable option and, depending on the ages of your children, can work out very well. If the kids are between eight and ten years old, the likelihood that they will do well in lessons is increased. Depending on the maturity, flexibility, and coordination levels of six- and seven-year-olds, they, too, can function well in ski school.

Tots, we think, need more individualized attention, and ski school is not normally the solution for them.

If you do choose ski school—for whatever reasons—don't leave it at that. When the lesson ends, ski with Roger. Let him boast about what he learned that day, and let him show you his progress.

However, the choice we prefer, that really is the premise of this book, is that you can teach your own children to ski.

Oh, of course there are prerequisites and caveats and all those things, but you can do it if you want to do it. If:

- you are a parent who enjoys doing things with your children;
- you can ski in complete control on intermediate (blue square) trails;
- you can snowplow from top to bottom of a beginner slope and come to a complete, strong stop;
- you know the proper way to fall and, when you do, can get up without a struggle;
- you have a basic level of patience with your child;
- you enjoy giving encouraging words.

If your answer to all of the above questions was yes, then we have absolutely no doubt that you can teach your own Roger and Amy to ski.

What's more, we think you're going to find it an enriching, exciting, and thoroughly enjoyable experience. You will need to be proficient enough on skis so that you can pay more attention to Roger's and Amy's skiing than your own, but don't let that scare you. Give it a try anyway. Being patient and encouraging are the two most important attributes.

## LITTLE ONES NEED ONE-ON-ONE

One-on-one instruction is a necessity for teaching small children to ski. We can't say that enough times. Not only do they have an extremely limited attention span, they also have an amazing array of needs, none of which occur at either the same or any reasonably appropriate time.

Drinking hot chocolate, going to the bathroom, warming cold hands, resting tired bodies, wiping noses, and a myriad of other real or imagined needs or ailments are all part of toddlers and skiing. Instruction must be flexible. In a group, flexibility is very difficult.

Since children this age thrive on encouragement and praise, individualized attention makes it possible to reinforce successes readily while immediately helping to correct mistakes. Keeping Roger's mind on the task he's trying to accomplish is no simple feat, but the regular reinforcement via praise helps turn the trick.

The opposite is true in a group situation. While Roger has picked up a task quite well, Jessica hasn't got it yet—for entirely different reasons. When the instructor starts helping Jessica, Roger becomes confused. It goes on and on.

**Children have an amazing array of
needs requiring your attention.**

Who besides you is more in tune with your child's individual needs? No one. Will Roger, Jessica, or Amy feel more secure and comfortable with a ski instructor than with you? Of course not.

That moment when Roger skis the beginner's slope all by himself for the very first time will be a rare, cherished time you will never forget.

## INDEPENDENCE COMES AT
## AGES SIX TO EIGHT

When the kids get to be six to eight, they become more and more independent and they don't require quite as much help in getting into their skis, walking on them, or getting up when they fall. They're more social now, and they depend on mom and dad less than they did as tots. Yet, there are distinct and sometimes not so subtle differences between six- to seven-year-olds and eight- to ten-year-olds.

Independence is certainly setting in at ages six and seven, but they still want to know mom or dad is nearby. We've seen parents drop their kids off at the Cochrans' Ski Area for a lesson that's supervised and skiing that isn't. Though they are certainly capable of skiing and enjoying it at ages six and seven, we've watched them cry at lunch, call home, or need special comforting by other adults. Independent? Sure, but there are times when parental reassurance is necessary.

Yet, if six-year-old Amy is mature, in good physical shape, and coordinated, she may do just fine in ski school. Either way, at this age they need lots of involvement from you.

When they get to be eight, nine, and ten years old, they make friends and they ski together. They generally do well with group instruction at this age and it doesn't take very long to master the basics of skiing, perhaps only a few hours. In fact, if given the opportunity, they could develop an interest in racing and competition.

**Group insruction works well with eight- to ten-year-olds.**

So, let's recap and put the age groups and group versus parental instruction into perspective.

Ski school provides a good social experience with no parent-child conflicts for three- to-five-year-olds.

Parental instruction, on the other hand, means individualized needs can be met, it's easier to keep kids happy and interested, encouragement is individualized, and progress is quicker. Obviously, security and comfort levels are raised, and there is a rewarding family experience budding.

The same is true for six- to seven-year-olds, though you can add learning more independence as a value in ski school. That need for reassurance should be noted when teaching them yourselves and added to the list of values.

Skiing with friends is important at ages eight to ten, and with independence increasing, ski school can work fine. Once again, however, progress is faster on an individualized basis.

# THREE

# GETTING READY TO SKI

Having the proper ski equipment makes all the difference in the world in helping a youngster learn to ski. We have some suggestions, but don't stop there.

Read the latest ski magazines, talk to the experts in your local ski shop, and ask instructors at the mountain. There are plenty of sources of good, current information.

The first decision that has to be made is whether it's better to rent ski equipment or to purchase it outright. The answer depends on your approach to the sport.

If you've made up your mind you are going to teach Jessica to ski, then buying her equipment is essential. But if you only plan on an occasional outing and you're not convinced Jessica is going to take to the sport, then rent for the time being.

Sure, buying equipment can be expensive, but many ski shops offer trade-in programs. When Jessica grows out of it next season, you simply trade it in for the next size.

If Jessica's younger brother, Douglas, is next in line, chances are Jessica's equipment will be just right for him. And don't forget to check out the end-of-season sales at most every ski shop and ski resort.

There are plenty of springtime bargains, and careful shopping at the right time of year is a great way to cut costs.

Sometimes, buying used ski equipment can help with the budget, but do be careful and make sure everything is in good working order. Have all bindings checked before using them. Look for ski swaps at clubs, churches, ski shows, and even at ski shops.

Weigh your options carefully: if you buy, you know the equipment is brand-new and in great shape. The downside is, of course, cost. The advantages to buying used equipment come on the cost side, but good skis and boots are hard to locate and there is indeed a wear-and-tear factor to consider.

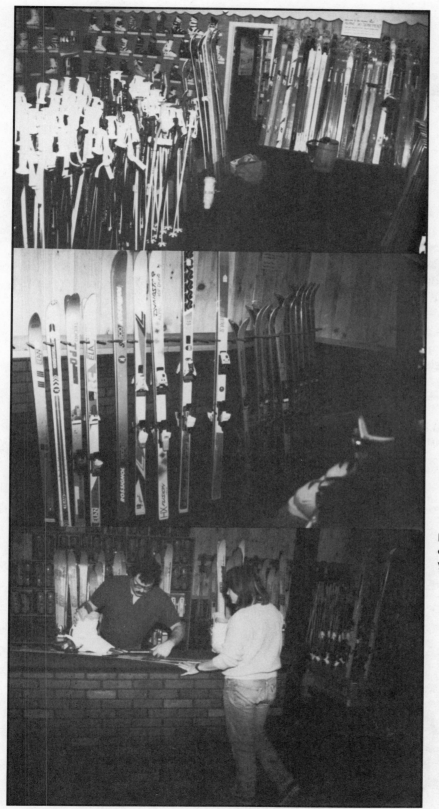

There's a vast array of new equipment on display at your local ski shop.

Used equipment costs less, but you need to be sure it's in good condition.

Rental equipment offers low initial costs but gets expensive the more you ski.

With rental equipment there is a low initial cost, but the disadvantage is having to go to the rental shop each time you head for the slopes. Besides, the meter is running each time you ski.

## TIPS ON BUYING SKIS

There are many ski shops that specialize in children's equipment; be sure to ask around. The ski you choose should have a soft flex. To test the flex, just hold the tip of the ski with one hand and put the tail against your instep. Then push on the middle of the ski with your other hand. Imagine that the pressure you are exerting is the same force Jessica will put on the ski. Could she exert that force?

Today's skis are designed to turn when pressure is applied; you don't have to muscle them around turns like we did in the days of wooden skis.

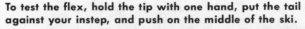

To test the flex, hold the tip with one hand, put the tail against your instep, and push on the middle of the ski.

Most ski companies build their children's models with these factors in mind. A number of companies manufacture skis specifically for kids, and among them are Rossignol, Atomic, K2, Techno Pro, Fisher, Blizzard, and Dynastar.

Whatever you do, be sure and get *regular* downhill, alpine skis for your tot. Don't put Doug on a pair of cross-country skis or, worse, on a pair of those plastic toys; that's a built-in disadvantage to the learning process.

When we learned to ski in the fifties, the skis were wooden and had no edges. We slipped our pack boots into the strap attached to the ski. Today that all seems like the Dark Ages, because the advances in ski manufacturing and technology have been remarkable.

Some children's skis have fish scales or a small patch of fur on the base in the middle of the ski, making it easier to walk with the skis on. However, the ski tends to be stiffer, making turning more difficult. Once Jessica gets more accomplished, this feature will actually slow the skis down.

Ideally you could use the fish scales for teaching walking and sidestepping and then switch to regular ski bases when it's time to teach turning. Since that's not practical for most families, use your own judgment or get advice from your ski shop.

The last ski decision is one of length. We follow the rule that the ski should be about head high—up to the chin for beginners and to the top of the head for more accomplished youngsters.

Since Douglas has never skied before, just stand the skis on end. They are just right if they come up to his chin. The longer skis offer smoother rides when the skier goes faster.

There are more choices for six- to ten-year-olds, and they are divided into three categories: junior recreational skis, junior sport skis, or junior racing skis. The ability levels break just as one might suspect, with beginners doing fine in recreational models, intermediate or better skiers enjoying the sport skis, and racers and experts using the racing series.

The recreational and sport skis are more stable for beginners and intermediates, and they tend to be less expensive than racing models, as well. But they are harder to turn.

Our recommendation is that children will progress quicker with sport or racing skis. They are going to learn fast anyway, going from raw beginner to the advanced intermediate stages, and at faster speeds, these skis are easier to turn.

A beginner in this age group should use skis that reach the top of his head. If he is a bit stronger for his age, then a little bit longer ski could help. A more experienced skier can handle a ski taller than his head.

A beginner should use skis that are shorter, coming about to the top of his head.

A more experienced or stronger skier can handle a ski that is a bit longer.

## BOOTS, BINDINGS, AND POLES

How boots fit is very important. For example, if the boots fit too tightly on Jimmy, his circulation is decreased and that means he'll have cold and uncomfortable feet.

If his boots are too loose, performance is hampered. His foot will move long before the boot does. Ski boots are designed to move the ski.

When you go to a reliable ski shop, the sales force will know how to fit boots properly. If you are doing it yourself at a sale or swap or simply working on a pair that Jessica outgrew, but might work fine for Doug, here are some guidelines that will help.

A boot with a good forward lean is important.

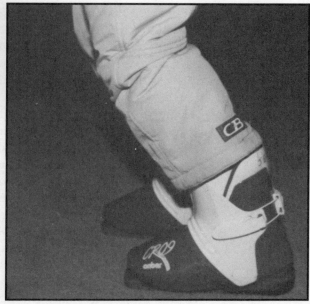

The child should be able to push the front of the boot easily.

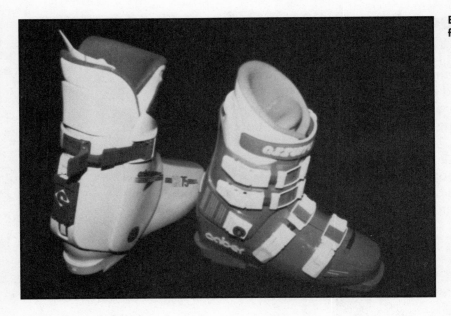

Boots come in rear- and front-entry models.

First, take out the inner boot (called the bladder). Most boots will come apart this way. Then, place Jimmy's foot in the bladder, making sure his heel is all the way back. Check to see if his toes have enough room to move. Once the boot is on, he should be able to wiggle his toes. Then just give the rest of the foot a feel to be sure it's comfortable.

Put the bladder back into the shell and put the boot on Doug. Have him kick his heel back and then just buckle up.

If you can put your hand down the back of the boot, it's too big. Likewise, when you hold the boot on the floor, Jimmy should not be able to lift his heel inside the boot. Heel fillers can be a remedy.

Companies making children's boots include Rossignol, Salomon, Nordica, Dolomite, Raichle, Lange, Technica, and Heierling.

Some people believe that boots are the single most important piece of equipment the skier has. When Doug is comfortable in the boot, he'll probably be comfortable on his skis, too.

Ask at the ski shop about the right kind of binding for Doug. There are lots of factors, and certified technicians at the shops know the perfect bindings for size and ability levels. Most attend the Skiing Mechanics Workshops each fall for the latest information.

An improperly adjusted binding makes learning to ski frustrating, so take the time to have it done correctly. Binding companies with products specifically made for children include Marker, Salomon, Tyrolia, Geze, and Look.

The bladder will easily come out of most boots.

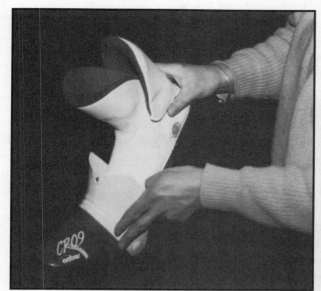

Put the bladder back into the boot, slip the foot in, and kick the heel back.

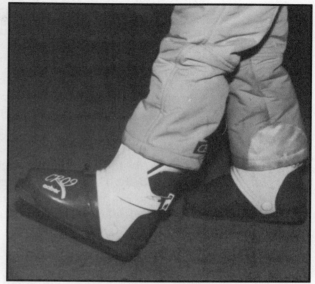

Put the foot in the bladder and check it for fit.

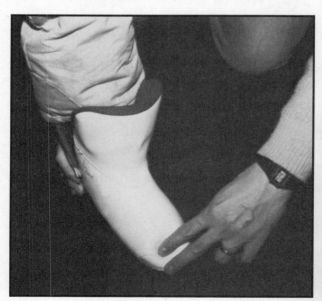

If you can put your hand down the back of the boot, it's too big.

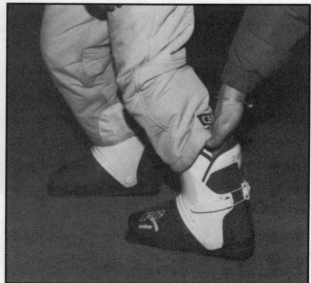

Now about poles: Barbara Ann remembers a race at Waterville Valley, New Hampshire, in 1969, when U.S. Ski Team member Cathy Nagel won a major event after dropping her pole at the start of the course. This incident is a good example of the fact that a pole (or poles) are not necessary. In truth, poles for beginners can hinder rather than help. Poles are used to help maintain a skier's balance, to skate across a section of flat terrain, and to help unload from a lift. For beginners and tots, they generally just get in the way. Skiing with Jimmy will be much easier for both of you if you forget about poles for a while.

We often see kids throw mild fits because they can't use poles "just like the big kids do." If that happens, give Jimmy the poles to try. He'll discard them quickly enough on his own. Older children should be taught without poles, too. They'll generally decide on their own when they want to begin using them.

At some point, though, a youngster will need poles. To determine the proper length of poles, ask your child to turn the pole

To determine proper length, hold poles upside down, gripping below the basket.

The upper and lower arm should form a ninety-degree angle.

upside down and grip it just below the basket. His upper and lower arm should form a ninety-degree angle.

Don't get carried away with having Doug's skis waxed to perfection. Hot waxing is fine when he's more of an accomplished skier, but for now, just stick a wax bar in your pocket and give the skis a shot when things are moving slowly.

Here's how to grip the pole correctly for skiing.

## CLOTHING

Sometimes the biggest difference between a happy camper and a miserable skier is the way he's dressed.

Doug will do very well if his clothing fits loosely yet warmly. Dressing up like a penguin, bundled tightly, makes it hard to move.

Layered clothing serves lots of purposes. The body can breathe while warm air is trapped. If it gets too warm, it's easy to remove layers.

Be sure to provide insulated top and bottom underwear for that inner layer. There's little bulk and the insulation is valuable. Don't forget a turtleneck, because lots of warmth can be lost with an exposed neck. A sweater completes the inner layer.

The outer layer should include a parka and bib warm-ups. A one-piece suit is great for tots. Both guard against snow sneaking through the gap at the waist when Jimmy takes his falls.

Keep socks to a minimum. Remember, ski boots provide lots more insulation than regular walking boots, so one or two medium-weight socks will keep those feet warm.

Insulated top and bottom underwear and socks are important.

Don't forget that turtleneck.

A sweater completes the inner
layer and bib warm-ups
start up the outer layer.

With the addition of the parka,
neckwarmer, and hat,
the outer layer is complete.

Body heat is lost through the head, and ears—especially the earlobes—are targets for frostbite. Find a hat that will stay on and covers the ears. Some children's hats are made with a built-in earflap that ties under the chin. These are perfect, particularly for younger children.

Barbara Ann always insisted that her hands got cold in gloves, so in 1972, when most World Cup racers wore gloves, she just went ahead and wore her mittens. In fact, when she won her Olympic Gold Medal, she was wearing mittens. We used to laugh about it, because sales of mittens went up all over the world.

A neck warmer is nice to have for those cold, windy days. It accomplishes the same thing as a scarf, but there are no loose ends to dangle and get caught on lifts. Tube-shaped neck warmers can be used to cover just the neck or, if it's really cold on a chair lift or while skiing, to cover the lower face.

Tots don't require goggles, but older children need them on windy, snowy days. Small children are going at such slow speeds that they usually aren't bothered by wind or snow in their faces, although they will probably want them so they can look like real skiers. When the kids get to be six to ten, they're spending more time outside and the goggles not only help them with their visibility, they tend to keep their faces warmer.

**Add a hat with earflaps.**

Once a child is dressed warmly, you can start putting on the actual skiing equipment. It's one thing to have all the equipment on hand; sometimes it's quite another to get Doug into it.

Let's start with boots. The warmer they are, the easier it will be for you to get them on, and the warmer they'll stay on Doug. Whatever you do, don't leave the boots in the car the night before. Are Doug's socks wrinkle free? We've seen lots of kids complain about sore feet, only to discover the cause was wrinkled socks.

**Are socks wrinkle free?**

The next subject is so silly we hesitate to mention it. But since we've seen it happen more than once, we'll do it anyway.

Be sure each boot is on the right foot! With rear-entry boots, for example, it is sometimes difficult to tell right from left. If you're confused, just look for the shape of the sole.

OK, all dressed? Find a flat area outside where Jimmy's skis won't slide. Place the skis side by side in the snow, making sure there is no ice or snow built up on the bottom of his boot and between the toe and heel of the binding. If there's any snow there, the equipment won't function properly.

Doug should place his foot—toe first—into the binding. He'll need lots of help at first, but he'll catch on soon and be proud of his independence.

Make a visual check to be sure the binding is on correctly (his toe shouldn't be crooked and his heel should be firmly in place).

Now it's time to ski.

# YOUR SKIER'S CHECKLIST: CHAPTER THREE

## GETTING DRESSED

### INNER LAYER

- ☐ Insulated long underwear tops tucked into bottoms
- ☐ Turtleneck tucked in, too
- ☐ Regular pants for really cold days
- ☐ Warm sweater
- ☐ One or two pair of medium-weight socks

### OUTER LAYER

- ☐ Parka and bib warm-ups (or one-piece suit)
- ☐ Hat with earflaps that ties under chin
- ☐ Mittens with long cuffs and Velcro fasteners or gloves with insulation
- ☐ Neck warmer

## GETTING READY TO SKI

### EQUIPMENT

- ☐ Soft-flex skis
- ☐ Length: to chin for beginning tots, top of head for more experienced tots and beginning six- to ten-year-olds, up to a few inches above head for more experienced six- to ten-year-olds and stronger youngsters
- ☐ Boot with a slightly forward lean
- ☐ Boot that fits snugly with heel held down; toes wiggle
- ☐ Bindings, checked by a certified ski technician, with ski brakes
- ☐ Poles (forget them for beginners)

### WAXING

- ☐ Bar of wax for use if snow is sticky

### PUTTING IT ON

- ☐ Keep boots warm until ready for use
- ☐ Keep socks wrinkle free
- ☐ Buckles always face the outside on boots
- ☐ Clear boot of snow and ice before stepping into binding
- ☐ Clear snow and ice between binding, toe, and heel
- ☐ Put toe in binding first, then heel
- ☐ Make a visual check of boot in binding

# FOUR

# GETTING ACQUAINTED WITH THE SKIS

When Lindy's Jessica was really little, she used to "ski" around the living room rug with her skis and boots on. When she was two, the summertime front lawn made ideal skiing terrain. It was fun, and it provided extra benefits in terms of practice time and building confidence.

Having skis underfoot is certainly not an everyday feeling. It's foreign to us all. We'll show you how the getting-to-know-you process works with skis and how games, fun, and encouragement play important roles.

Once again, there are differences between a tot and an older child, so the instruction for each will be somewhat different.

Timmy will be our three- to five-year-old would-be skier. Like all others in his age group, Timmy is very much dependent on his mom and dad, so you'll have to have lots of hands-on activities where you physically move him into the correct positions.

You'll have to watch your language, too. Explain ideas in very simple terms and encourage Timmy to use his imagination.

Jessica will be our six- to seven-year-old skier. She's more independent than Timmy and can do tasks on her own that he's not ready to do, such as putting on her own skis and walking on them.

She'll require some hands-on help, but for the most part she'll be able to get into the right position by imitating yours.

Still, be sure to use simple explanations and terms and challenge her imagination.

Tom is our eight- to ten-year-old and he's all set for quick progress. He's independent and doesn't require much physical contact. Just demonstrate a movement and he'll imitate it. Have Tom follow you. He has a longer attention span and he's able to listen attentively to instructions. He likes to play games, too, but none of that baby stuff we are using with Timmy.

To make it easy to understand, let's first talk about instructing Timmy (ages three to five) and then we'll deal with Jessica (ages six to seven) and Tom (ages eight to ten).

36

There will be plenty of hands-on
efforts where you will physically
move him into the correct position.

Older children can listen better
and can imitate well.

## TAKING A WALK WITH TIMMY

OK, let's take a walk. You don't need to be on skis if it's easier for you to walk with Timmy. He should be all set to go. You won't need a big area, but be sure it's flat. Look in your yard or at the park. The flatter the spot, the easier it will be for Timmy to learn to walk on skis without sliding backward or forward.

Once Timmy is outside on the snow on his new skis, start the steady stream of encouragement that is going to be your trademark.

"You're on your skis! Look at Timmy, my skier! Now, let's see you slide!"

Let Timmy experiment a bit with the feel of skis on his feet. He'll probably try lifting his skis as if he were lifting a foot to walk.

A common mistake: this child is lifting each ski to walk, instead of sliding his skis on the snow.

When he does, just encourage him to slide one ski forward and then slide the other one up to meet the first. If he's having trouble understanding, try talking about sliding his boot, rather than the ski. Ultimately, we want Timmy to slide one ski forward and the other *beyond* the first one, ending up with a shuffling motion.

A child begins to slide forward on the snow. Here, feet are together...

...slide one ski forward...

...feet are together again, then...

...slide the other ski forward until . . .

. .feet are together once more.

Balance is a real consideration at this point. The front-to-back balance is the relationship of the upper body to the front or the back of the skis. This balance is usually the most critical.

None of us—let alone Timmy—is used to having our feet move ahead of our upper body. Timmy might begin to fall on the backs of his skis. If he does, remind him to bring his head forward as he slides his skis.

Let him practice on his own for a while. He'll adjust very quickly, probably quicker than you did!

The side-to-side balance is the relationship of the upper body to the outside of each ski. This balance probably won't bother

Timmy much because the skis provide a stabilized platform, but he might topple over sideways a few times at first.

Just pick him up, offer plenty of encouragement, and send him on his way again. The more time Timmy spends on skis, the more comfortable he'll feel.

Let's play a couple of games with him now.

Choo-choo train is a favorite that works. Walk around in front of Timmy, and pretend to be the train's engine.

Have him follow in your tracks and make all the necessary choo-choo train sounds. Let Timmy be the engine from time to time.

Follow the leader is another way to learn. First you, then Timmy, can lead the other all around the yard, park, or snowy area creating all kinds of imaginary ski adventures. Go through the forest hunting for bears or round up the horses into the corral. Let Timmy use his imagination.

Once Timmy is comfortable on his skis, the time has come to teach him to sidestep. Soon, and with a degree of frustration before he masters it, he'll be able to move up an incline without sliding back down.

This, frankly, is a tough maneuver for a beginner to learn. Remember when you were learning it? Timmy doesn't have to do it in one try; it'll come over time. Have him attempt the sidestep, but help him along if he really gets frustrated.

**To begin the sidestep, the child should face both skis across the slope of the hill.**

The child lifts the uphill ski away from the downhill ski and plants it farther up the hill.

The child then lifts the downhill ski and places it next to the uphill ski.

Parents can help get the idea across by pushing his knee sideways into the hill, rolling the ski on edge.

You'll need a bit of an incline for your sidestepping lessons, but a front or backyard with a slight snowy incline should be fine. Timmy's skis should be facing across the hill's slope.

Ask Timmy to lift his *uphill* ski (point it out a few times and show him that it is the ski highest on the hill), and have him dig the upper edge of the ski into the snow up the hill from where the ski originated. You may have to demonstrate here.

Timmy should then lift the bottom ski and dig the upper edge of that ski into the snow next to the first one. You can help by pushing his knee sideways toward the hill, rolling the ski on edge. You might have to kneel down in the snow next to Timmy and physically lift his uphill ski boot, place it in the snow, and repeat the task with the second ski.

Variations in terrain can be deceiving to the eye, particularly the entry areas to lifts. These variations present all kinds of problems until the sidestep is mastered. So keep working on it.

A general rule of thumb on sidestepping is if the skis are sliding backward, the ski tips need to come down the hill in relation to the tails. If the skis are sliding forward, the ski tips need to come up the hill in relation to the tails.

The most common mistake Timmy and every other kid will make is failing to keep his skis perpendicular to the slope of the hill.

He'll start out fine, but then he'll reason that it's silly to keep sideways when his goal is to go *up* the hill. So he'll gradually bring his ski tips up the hill, allowing the skis to slide back down. Timmy

**Turning skis uphill is a common mistake.**

will understand if you explain that the idea is to walk *sideways* up the hill.

Let's play some more games that will help.

The marching band is great practice. Pretend you and Timmy are marching sideways up the hill. Have him pick up his skis and slam them back onto the snow. This is useful because he's learning to pick up his skis.

Slicing the snow helps teach sidestepping and using edges. Have Timmy experiment with using the edge of his ski to slice into the snow, leaving a straight mark. Show him the difference between the marks left in the snow by a flat ski and one that has edged.

This can be a frustrating time for both of you, and sidestepping isn't your number-one priority in teaching Timmy to ski. Help him along if he's having difficulty. Pick him up if you need to. As he gets more comfortable on his skis, it will be easier.

Above all else, keep a smile on his face. And on yours, too.

## IT'S DIFFERENT WITH OLDER CHILDREN

Teaching Jessica and Tom is different. Children from six to ten, as we've said, are more independent.

Jessica and Tom should begin by simply walking around on their skis. The goal is to get used to the skis sliding along, rather than lifting them, and to get used to the balance. If Tom is clumsy at first and the skis are sliding every which way but the right way, this stage will quickly pass. Depending on variables, he'll be comfortable somewhere between ten and thirty minutes.

The walking area, once again, does not need to be big, but it does need to be flat. There's little difference between working with Jessica (six to eight) and Tom (eight to ten) at this point. If they fall, help them up; if they need a shove, push them. They *will* need encouragement, so give it to them.

Demonstrate how to slide the skis along. Then let Jessica and Tom experiment with the feel of the skis on their feet. At first, they will try lifting one ski as if lifting up a foot to walk, but it won't take long to realize that won't work.

Encourage Jessica to slide one ski forward and then to slide the other one up to meet it. Once again, the ultimate idea is to slide the other ski *beyond* the first one, ending with that shuffling motion.

The first time the skis slide forward, Jessica might feel like she's just slipped on ice and her feet have scooted away. Laugh about it and reassure her the feeling is normal. She simply has to lean forward while the skis slide. The side-to-side balance is not generally a problem for this age group. On the flats, all Jessica has to do if she feels like she's going to fall over is to move a ski sideways. Show her how.

Follow the leader works well here, too. Lead Jessica around the area. Begin with a big circle, so she can gradually change directions and end up where she started.

Tom will love to play tag, and it's a great game once he's comfortable on skis. When Tom is it, try to slide out of his reach while he chases you. Once he touches you, you're it. You chase him until you catch him.

Jessica may need more help with learning the frustrating sidestep than Tom will, but before long, both will be doing fine.

Keep reminding them to dig in the uphill ski and then lift up the downhill ski and dig its upper edge into the snow, next to the first one.

Two common mistakes Jessica and Tom may make are taking too big a step and/or failing to keep their skis perpendicular to the slope. Encourage them to take baby steps rather than giant steps. Keep reminding them they are walking *sideways* up the hill.

Once Timmy, Jessica, and Tom have learned to sidestep twenty to thirty feet up an incline by themselves (or with a little bit of help), they are ready to ski.

So, let's go skiing.

# YOUR SKIER'S CHECKLIST: CHAPTER FOUR

## INSTRUCTING TOTS

### WALKING ON SKIS

☐ Walking on skis, sliding them back and forth

☐ Getting used to front and back balance

☐ Getting used to side balance

### GAMES TO PLAY

☐ Choo-choo train

☐ Follow the leader

### SIDESTEPPING

☐ Skis are perpendicular to the slope of the hill

☐ Uphill ski is lifted up the hill

☐ Downhill ski is lifted up to uphill ski

☐ Skis stay *sideways* to the hill at all times

### MORE GAMES TO PLAY

☐ The marching band

☐ Slicing the snow

## INSTRUCTING SIX-TO TEN-YEAR-OLDS

☐ The same as above for walking and sidestepping

### GAMES TO PLAY

☐ Follow the leader

☐ Tag

# SOMETHING SPECIAL WHEN THEY ARE UNDER THREE

Jessica started her ski career when she was just fifteen months old. She had great balance and loved it, right from the beginning. She was always skiing between Lindy's or Steve's legs or gliding into our waiting arms after a short distance on her own. She wore everybody out and we were always ready to quit before she was.

Timmy, her brother, didn't start until he was twenty months old. He didn't take to it like his sister did. He preferred hanging out in the lodge and earned his nickname, "the lodge lizard," because he was more interested in investigating what was hiding in lunch sacks than going outside and playing in the snow.

Weigh carefully the advantages and disadvantages of getting kids under the age of three into skiing.

Skiing with a toddler (as opposed to when they become a tot) has plenty of potential for becoming either a rewarding experience or a total disaster. One day, you and little Jennifer will have a wonderful time; the next day you'll wish you were home in front of the TV set.

Circumstances may vary, but generally speaking, the older the toddler, the better your chances. This is because communication is a problem with very young skiers. A one-year-old, for example, may be whining and crying and you have absolutely no idea why. A two-year-old, on the other hand, has a larger vocabulary and can express likes and dislikes better. Also, the muscular development of older children allows them to do more for themselves.

Your own skiing ability plays a very important role. If you are a beginner, we don't recommend your attempting to ski with Jennifer.

Accessibility to the slopes is an important factor. Long automobile trips will tire her out before she even gets to the snow. The more hassle free the arrival, the better your odds for a successful outing.

Keep your expectations to a minimum. There are definite limitations to the progress you can reasonably expect. Ski with Jennifer for parent-child participation and the beginnings of communication links, *not* to produce the hottest two-year-old wonder ever to hit the slopes.

Patience will become your biggest virtue. If you don't have it to begin with, try something else. Strap a pair of skis on their feet and be ready for anything!

If it's obvious that your skiing adventure could turn into a battle of wills, wait a year or so and try again. Don't force it.

Yet, if you do have the patience to deal with Jennifer's whims, go ahead and give it a try.

There are a number of advantages to teaching Jennifer to ski now. It gets you outside and is good exercise for both of you. It's something a parent and toddler can do together in winter, and there is indeed a wonderful sense of pride in each accomplishment.

On the downside, it can be very frustrating for both of you. Jennifer can't always communicate her needs, and a test of patience will develop. You may be doing all the skiing for her, and that's going to be hard on your back.

**There's a wonderful sense of pride in each accomplishment.**

Let's start with Jennifer at age one. If she can walk, she can ski. True enough, but you'll do most of the work.

Begin by skiing with her between your legs, giving her full support at all times. Even at age one, she's going to love going over bumps, so make sure you look for them.

All you can expect to accomplish is to give her a feeling for her skis gliding over snow, and hopefully you both will be having a good time.

As you ski more and more with her, she will begin to support more of her own weight. Let her ski a very short distance without your support at the bottom of a slope.

The best bet is to have another adult catch her shortly after you let go. It's very similar to when she took her first steps.

Here's a warning: at this age, Jennifer will fall face first without using her hands to break her fall. To protect her, keep the distances extremely short and her speed very slow.

## STILL SLOW AT AGE TWO

When Jennifer is starting at age two, you can expect a bit more progress, yet the best teaching tool you have is your patience. Progress will probably be very slow, but don't put on undue pressure to learn.

Again, start off with Jennifer between your legs. Before too long, she should be able to balance herself on her skis.

This is where the trouble starts. Jennifer has some balance but no concept of control. She will do everything in her power to stay on her feet as she goes faster and faster straight down the hill. She wants to ski by herself, yet she has no fear or control.

To help Jennifer ski safely, we use the tried-and-true falling-into-the-hill method (see next chapter). Two-year-olds have definite ideas about *not* wanting to fall. If she refuses to fall, try the harness aid we discuss in more detail in chapter 8.

If you use the harness, try to keep both yours and Jennifer's speed under control. Stay off advanced slopes; it's more difficult to manage. She should be kept on the harness until she can or will fall into the hill and can control her speed with a snowplow.

You can also work with her snowplow by skiing backward in front of her holding her tips. But, don't let her go by herself until she learns the right way to fall.

Again, keep your expectations in check.

It can still be fun, even with a harness.

A one-year-old can ski between your legs and hold most of her weight. She can balance by herself for short distances, and an older one-year-old might be able to ski with a harness.

A two-year-old can do anything a one-year-old can do, plus she will be able to transfer weight (without control), learn to fall the right way, turn with a snowplow, and perhaps ride a handle lift (such as a Mitey Mite) by herself.

If you understand the deepest meanings of the word *patience,* give it a whirl.

# YOUR SKIER'S CHECKLIST: CHAPTER FIVE

### CONSIDERATIONS

- ☐ Age of child
- ☐ Skiing ability of parent
- ☐ Accessibility of ski slopes
- ☐ Expectations for your child
- ☐ Your patience levels

### ONE-YEAR-OLD

- ☐ Ski with your child between your legs, giving full support
- ☐ Let your child ski a short distance alone

### TWO-YEAR-OLD

- ☐ Ski with your child between your legs
- ☐ Teach control, falling into the hill, and the snowplow turn
- ☐ Use a harness if your child doesn't understand control
- ☐ Teach your child to ride a handle lift, if one is available

# TIME TO SLIDE DOWNHILL

OK, now we know how to get up the hill. It's time we mastered getting *down* the hill.

The very first skill we teach a beginner after they've mastered walking and hiking uphill is how to fall, because every skier falls. Ask any novice skier—young or old—and the goal they are looking to attain is how *not* to fall! The fact of the matter, though, is that falling properly is a perfect way of putting on the brakes for a novice skier, before he or she is adept at stopping.

Naturally, there's the little matter of getting up from a fall and we'll deal with that here, too.

We'll discover the snowplow position and braking snowplow for six- to ten-year-olds (tots won't deal with the snowplow until later on).

Let's look at the *right way* of showing Douglas, age four, to fall.

## LEARN HOW TO FALL
## (AND HOW TO GET UP)

The Cochran method is known as falling into the hill. The uphill hip lands in the snow above the skis, if Doug is doing it properly.

The bottom of the skis are no longer flat against the snow, so now it's impossible for the skis to continue sliding and Doug can skid to a stop.

Look for a gentle slope. Have Doug stand still on his skis, facing you, while you demonstrate our falling-into-the-hill technique.

It's time to use yours and Doug's imagination now. Picture a dot or a heart on your uphill hip. Fall to the ground right on top of the dot, and break your fall with the hand that's closest to the snow.

Now, it's Doug's turn to try it. But before he does it, let's fire up his imagination and fantasize this scenario with him:

Point to the spot on the hip where the child should try to fall.

Fall into the hill, and break the fall with the hand closest to the snow.

The uphill hip lands in the snow above the skis while the bottom of the skis are no longer flat against the snow.

"I'm skiing down the hill. Oh, no! [Panic on your face.] I'm going faster and faster! Oh, no! I'm out of control! What am I going to do? I know! I've got to fall into the hill like this [demonstrate]. Now it's your turn to try it, Doug!"

Go through the fantasy again, switching "I'm" to Doug. Practice it several times, as long as his attention is there.

The most common wrong way kids fall is sitting down on the backs of the skis.

We can't tell you how many times we've heard well-meaning moms and dads spot their son or daughter out of control and scream in desperation, "Sit down! Sit down!" It may seem to be the natural response, but it isn't.

When a skier sits down on the backs of the skis, the skis continue moving downhill with little reduction of speed—sometimes even picking up speed. There is absolutely no control possible, which is dangerous.

The other common wrong way to fall is falling down the hill. Don't let this one happen either. The height of the fall is higher because the slope of the hill is going away from the skier. Falling downhill sends the head downhill first and, obviously, that's very dangerous.

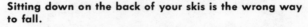

**Sitting down on the back of your skis is the wrong way to fall.**

Once Doug has the idea of falling into the hill, he needs to get comfortable with the concept of falling while his skis are sliding.

You and Doug should sidestep up a gentle slope, perhaps ten feet. If he hasn't mastered the sidestep totally yet, get him started and then push or carry him the rest of the way. We don't need him frustrated right now.

Once you reach the starting point, remind him about that imaginary dot or heart and demonstrate gliding down the slope a short way and falling into the hill, right on top of that dot. Now, turn around and have Doug try it.

The gliding and falling exercise is very important, and Doug needs to be fairly accomplished at it before going any further. Start each day on skis with a review of the glide and fall technique before doing anything else.

There's just no way we can overestimate the importance of this technique. It's the basis for everything else we do.

The next frustration you and Doug will encounter is getting up once he falls. Remember your own frustration when you were learning and trying to pick yourself up? Of course you do.

Doug is going to need lots of encouragement, and you should be quite willing to literally give him a helping hand. He's learning plenty of new skills right now, and we don't want to overwhelm him with what he views as impossible tasks piled upon impossible tasks.

Once Doug falls, have him lie on his back. Tell him to point his ski tips straight up in the air. Point your hands up in the air like you're signaling a touchdown.

Now, have Doug lay his skis side by side across the hill. Tell him to bend his knees and to put his *uphill* hand behind his rear and push up onto his knees and stand up.

Another way to get up after Doug gets his skis side by side across the hill is to have him push with his uphill hand so he is sitting on his haunches, almost a squatting position. He stands up from there.

Have Doug do what he can while keeping his frustration — and yours — to a minimum.

For example, let's say Doug is all tangled up in his skis and can't seem to get out by lying on his back. Just grab him under the armpits and lift him in the air so he can straighten out his skis. Otherwise, it will only get worse.

If Doug is having a hard time pushing up onto his knees, grab him firmly — but gently — by his jacket or upper arm and help him up.

This is going to take some time and patience on both your part and Doug's. Yet, before you know it, Doug will have developed

**56**

How do I get out of this mess?

Lie on back and point ski tips
straight up in the air.

Lay skis side by side across the hill.

Bend knees and put uphill hand behind rear.

Push up onto knees and stand up.

If all else fails and he's still tangled up, grab him under the armpits and lift him into the air.

muscles, coordination, and confidence and will be getting up from a fall all by himself.

You owe Doug a cup of hot chocolate and yourself a cup of coffee.

## FALLS IMPORTANT FOR OLDER KIDS, TOO

Let's look at falling for the older kids.

Amy, age six, and other novice skiers from her age group (six to ten), have little control over turning or stopping. Yet, she probably has the balance and can move quickly on skis. She needs to learn a quick and easy way to stop, no matter how much trouble she might find herself in. The solution is easy: the fall.

There is a right way to fall at this age and stage of skiing development. Amy's natural tendency, when she feels she is losing control, is to back away from where she's going.

Since Amy's feet are attached to her skis, she ends up just falling back and sitting on her tails. Since her skis can still glide, she obviously just goes faster.

Again, here's the fall-into-the-hill technique we talked about with Doug. It's just as important for Amy. The body (spot on hip) hitting the snow will cause her to stop because the bottoms of the skis are no longer flat on the snow. Therefore, she can't continue her slide and she'll skid to a stop.

OK, you're ready to teach Amy to fall. Stand on the hill and face her. If we were scriptwriters, here's how we'd have you phrase it:

"You're not going to believe this, Amy, but the first thing I'm going to teach you today is how to fall! The reason I'm going to teach you how to fall is because *anytime you get going too fast* [stress this], you can always stop by *falling*.

"Amy, there is a *right* way and a *wrong* way to fall. I'm going to show you how people who are scared fall. Tell me if you think it is the right way or the wrong way to fall. [Demonstrate falling back and sitting on your skis.] Was that the right way to fall? The wrong way? Good! It's the wrong way.

"To fall the *right* way, we have to fall into the hill. Which way is up the hill? [Have Amy point up the hill.] Good! Imagine you have a dot (or a heart) on your *uphill* hip. Where is your dot? [Amy points to it.] Good! When you ski across the hill, fall right on that dot."

Demonstrate and practice.

Once Amy gets comfortable with falling and thoroughly

understands the right way to accomplish it, it's time to work on gliding and falling.

Ask Amy to sidestep up a slight incline about twenty feet. Before she begins to practice gliding and falling, demonstrate the skills required yourself a few times. Then, have Amy point her skis across the hill and slightly down to begin gliding.

After she's slid about five feet, yell "Fall!" Amy should plop down on her dot on the uphill hip. When she does it right, offer lots of praise.

Practice to the left and to the right for as long as you can keep her attention to the task.

There is no difference in getting up for this age group than the younger kids. Lie on the back, ski tips up in the air and skis side by side across the hill; with hand behind rear, push up onto knees and stand up. The other way works well, too: skis are side by side across the hill; push on the uphill hand and sit on haunches. Stand up from there.

## AMY LEARNS THE SNOWPLOW

Staying with Amy's age group (not Doug's or tots), let's help them learn the snowplow position.

There are two reasons for teaching the snowplow, and we Cochrans think they are extremely valuable. The snowplow is synonymous with control, and it's a fine preparation for learning to turn.

Amy can learn to ski in control and can quickly slow down and stop by using the snowplow. Our motto at the Cochran's Ski Area is Ski in Control!

The snowplow position also prepares a novice for turning. If the skis are on edge and bent in an arc, today's manufacturing technology allows them to turn.

The skis are already on edge in the snowplow. To get them to bend in an arc, all Amy has to do is to add weight to the *outside* ski. Once these two tasks are completed, the skis will turn.

Back when we learned to ski with wooden skis and screw-in edges, we really had to muscle the skis around and it was hard work. Maybe that's why we never had trouble sleeping at night!

Yet as simple as it sounds, the snowplow isn't a natural position. It's awkward for everyone and takes some getting used to. Like everything else we're talking about in the early stages, learning the snowplow can be frustrating. Be patient with Amy. Offer encouragement and gentle reminders.

Amy's skis form a V or a triangle in the snowplow position. Her tips are together and her tails are apart. Amy pushes her knees toward each other (the center) so that both skis are put on edge. Children Amy's age may need help stabilizing the position, and her hands can be placed on her knees if necessary.

**Here's the snowplow position close up.**

**Full view of the snowplow position.**

Let's teach her.

Amy should sidestep twenty feet up the hill, just like she did when working on gliding and falling. Ask her to point her skis downhill, and be ready to catch her if she begins to slide.

Stand in front of her and support her by holding her tips. Tell her to put her skis into a V with the tips together and the tails apart.

Amy might feel the urge to lean forward and hang onto your back. That's common. Stop and reassure her that since you are holding her skis, she won't go anywhere until you let her.

**Stand in front, hold tips, push tails out.**

**Clinging to your jacket is common. Reassure the child that all's well.**

Don't let her move until she's got her hands on her knees and is supporting herself.

While she is standing still, ask her to make a bigger V by pushing her tails out more. Don't use the term "push out your heels," because it will confuse her and she'll likely push out her entire foot.

You may have to help the first time by actually grabbing her heels and pushing them out. The younger kids (six and seven) usually need this kind of help.

Once Amy understands how to push her tails out, let go of her tips and move down a few feet. Tell her to come toward you but remain in the snowplow position. If her skis come together, grab hold of her tips and ask her to push them out again. Keep reminding her the snowplow is the position she should be in.

As Amy skis toward you, ask her to make bigger and bigger Vs and then come to a stop. She'll soon realize that she can slow down by making a bigger V and can actually stop by pushing her tails out wide.

Move down the hill again and repeat the exercise. Practice until Amy can ski forward, slow down, and stop, all while maintaining the snowplow position.

The next step in learning to ski for this age group is braking the snowplow.

**Let go of the tips and move in front of the child.**

Encourage making a bigger V.

## PUTTING BRAKES ON THE SNOWPLOW

Amy will begin with a snowplow, just as she learned it, allowing the skis to run together. Then she'll brake by pushing her skis back into a snowplow.

Same drill as before. Ask Amy to sidestep about twenty feet up the hill. Demonstrate how to brake a snowplow yourself before she tries it. Begin snowplowing straight down the hill. Let your skis come together and then push them back into the snowplow to slow down.

Now have Amy try it. Stand about fifteen to twenty feet below her this time, and have her move toward you in a snowplow. Have her skis run together (she'll pick up speed), and then push her tails out (she should be slowing down) and encourage her to get back into a snowplow.

"Wider, wider, wider, wider—now stop!" She should be able to stop when you tell her to do so. It will take some practice—doesn't everything?—but soon Amy will be comfortable in the snowplow position. She'll also be comfortable gliding, braking, and stopping.

It won't be long now until she's riding the lift and turning.

The first step in braking the
snowplow is the snowplow position.

Skis should run together
and pick up speed.

She then pushes her tails out and returns to a snowplow.

# YOUR SKIER'S CHECKLIST: CHAPTER SIX
## INSTRUCTING TOTS

### FALLING

☐ Fall into the hill

☐ Fall onto an imaginary dot or heart on the uphill hip

☐ Describe a fantasy scenario

### GLIDING AND FALLING

☐ Sidestep up ten feet

☐ Glide down the hill

☐ Fall into the hill

☐ Review each day you ski

### GETTING UP

☐ Give a helping hand

☐ Have child lie on back and flip skis over

☐ Have child push up on knees and stand up

# YOUR SKIER'S CHECKLIST: CHAPTER SIX

## INSTRUCTING SIX-
## TO TEN YEAR-OLDS

### FALLING

☐ Fall into the hill

☐ Fall on the imaginary dot on uphill hip

☐ Demonstrate the right way to fall

### GLIDING AND FALLING

☐ Sidestep up twenty feet

☐ Glide across and down the hill

☐ Fall into the hill

☐ Practice gliding to both the right and left

### GETTING UP

☐ Same as above

### SNOWPLOW POSITION

☐ Skis form a V with tips together, tails apart

☐ Knees in, hands on knees

☐ Skis up on edge

☐ May have to support tips

### BRAKING SNOWPLOW

☐ Demonstrate first

☐ Begin in snowplow

☐ Skis run together

☐ Push tails out to slow down and stop

# SEVEN

# GETTING A LIFT OUT OF SKIING

Now that we're just about out of the climb-up-twenty-feet-and-snowplow-down stage, it's time to make our lives a bit easier by riding lifts. Unfortunately for kids, the surface lift is becoming an endangered species. In far too many ski areas, the surface lift has become extinct, giving way to high-tech, high-speed detachable lifts that are difficult for children to ride on their own.

If you can do your early skiing where there are surface lifts (and thankfully, several areas have added Mitey Mites recently), you'll find it's much easier and more fun to learn for both of you. It's warmer, too. If not, so be it. Take on the high tech!

The biggest virtue of surface lifts is that they bring your skier up the hill with his or her skis gliding on the snow. Speed is controlled by the lifts, and the kids get plenty of gliding practice.

Perhaps you live close enough to Richmond, Vermont (near Burlington), and the Cochran Ski Area. Our lifts are low tech and we're proud of it. Maybe that's why we're so successful with kids.

Actually, we have a 1,600-foot T-bar where two kids at a time can go up the hill; a 1,100-foot rope tow (just like the one we learned to ski on); a 450-foot Mitey Mite; and a short, 500-foot rope tow.

The newest of the new—the detachable quad lifts— are the best of the aerial lifts for learning, since they slow to a snail's pace for loading, before whisking you up the hill. Many of the big destination or vacation areas are converting to this variety. Vail, for example, has six of them. But we recommend surface lifts first, so let's show you how to teach your kids to ride them.

Our first choice is the Mitey Mite. You may have to search around to find one, but it's worth the effort. On the other hand, just in our northern Vermont neighborhood alone, Mitey Mites can be found at Smuggler's Notch, Bolton Valley, and Stowe.

The Mitey Mite is a slow handle lift that is easy to get on and off. The skier holds onto the handle and is pulled up the hill. The sensation is similar to slow-speed water skiing.

No matter what lift you are riding, get instructions on how to load yourself and your child before you get to the loading ramp. After you get the verbal instructions, watch for a while.

A lift—no matter how simple—is an intimidating piece of machinery to a child. So try your best to avoid a bad initial experience because it can set a skier's confidence back many days.

The Mitey Mite at the Cochran Ski Area is set up so the lift attendant can stop the lift for beginning skiers to load.

Let's work with Roger today. Put him between your legs and step into the tracks parallel to the lift. Don't rush; take your time.

**Always check out instructions before loading any new lift.**

Watch as others load onto a lift.

On any surface lift, be sure yours and your child's skis
are pointed straight up the hill.

Be sure that both yours and Roger's skis are pointing straight up the hill, parallel to the line of the lift cable. Turn around and hold your hand up, motioning to the lift attendant to stop the Mitey Mite for you.

Once the handle has stopped near you (you may have to glide forward or back a bit to meet the handle), hold the handle horizontally with your hands spread apart from each other, knuckles up.

Roger should hold onto the handle from the beginning, even though you are doing most of the work for him at this point.

You and Roger should have your knees slightly bent for a balanced position. Hold your knees together to support him and to keep him from slipping between your legs.

Try to relax. Roger has some time in grade now on skis and has some decent balance, so he can do some of the work. Don't put him in a vise so he is doing nothing.

**Both parent and child hold onto the Mitey Mite handle.**

Roger's arms should be bent at the elbows. While you are riding, fill his ears with praise and encouragement. Have fun. Explain how and where you will be getting off the lift.

"When we reach that flat spot at the top, we will be letting go of the handle."

When you get to that point, simply let go of the handle, pick Roger up, and step to the side. The key to getting off any surface lift (Mitey Mite, T-bar, rope tow) is stepping to the side as quickly as possible once you let go.

Once he is more stable and confident, he will become more and more independent in riding the Mitey Mite.

Each time you ride up together, gradually slide back, assuring him you are still close by him. Slide back by grabbing the cable with both hands, one behind the other, as if you were climbing a rope. When you get near the top, remind Roger that you'll tell him when to let go of the handle and sidestep to the side. After a few times helping him, he'll be able to do this by himself.

Once he can ride it by himself, the next step is to have him start off at the bottom by himself. Follow behind a few runs by hanging onto the cable, then he'll be fine without you.

Here's a little side tip that will help: tell Roger it's OK if he falls off the Mitey Mite. Just *let go* of the handle.

When Jessica was two years old, she was riding the Mitey Mite between our legs. Soon she spotted her cousin, Roger, then three years old, riding the lift by himself. Her Aunt Marilyn tried to help her up the lift but she screamed the whole way.

We finally figured out she was yelling, "I want to ride by myself!" We let her. This was a full month before she could ski down by herself.

The final Mitey Mite skill to master is getting on a moving lift. Position Roger in the tracks with both skis parallel to the lift cable. Have him turn around, reach out with both hands, and grab the handle as it goes by. Keep up those important words of praise.

Imitation is important. Roger can learn a great deal by watching others board a Mitey Mite.

## RIDING OTHER SURFACE LIFTS

T-bars and even an occasional J-bar are fairly common lifts and do many of the same things for Roger's skiing practice.

Instead of hanging onto a handle in front of you, a T-shaped bar rests behind his bottom and pulls him up the hill.

The most common single mistake made with T-bars is sitting down on the bar. Roger simply stands up and lets the bar guide him up the slope.

For learning purposes, you and Roger should be in the same position as with the Mitey Mite. He's between your legs, both sets of skis pointing uphill.

Instead of hanging onto a handle, Roger hangs onto your legs. Once you're prepared in the tracks, turn your upper body to the center to grasp the bar as it comes up behind you. There is normally a lift attendant to guide the T or J toward you.

Talk to Roger. It's important. Tell him what's happening at all times. When you get to the top, slip the T or J off from behind and toss it to the side. A platter pull lift works in similar ways to the T-bar, except a disc on a pole goes between your legs. It's not as easy to teach to ride as a T-bar.

The simplest lift of all is the tried-and-true rope tow, where you hang onto the rope and you're pulled up the hill. Thankfully, some of the largest destination ski areas have one or two of these

**It's much easier for both of you to ride a T-bar
if you place the child between your legs.**

still functioning for beginners. We all used to joke about one arm becoming longer than the other from riding the rope tows, but they remain a fun way to travel.

You should be very familiar with the ins and outs of rope tow riding before you tackle it with Roger. Take some trial runs to get the feel of it, if it's been awhile since you've ridden one.

The key skill is to *gently squeeze* the rope tighter and tighter. As you squeeze, the rope will pull you faster and faster until you reach the same speed as the rope. Hold on until you reach the top, let go, and ski to the side.

With Roger between your legs, proceed up the rope tow as you have practiced by yourself. Have him hang onto your legs at first. Keep your legs close together and be sure to guard against Roger slipping through.

**Keep your child between your legs on the rope tow.**

After Roger has been up and down a number of times and has some confidence, then teach him to do it by himself. You may have to hold the rope to his height, but otherwise it's the same for him as it was for you.

Depending on his strength or the difficulty of the rope or the incline (or snow conditions), he may or may not be able to hold on all the way to the top. Just stay close behind for a while, in case he needs a gentle push.

**When your child is ready to try the rope tow on his own, stay close behind in case he needs a nudge.**

## RIDING HIGH

The most common lifts are known as chair lifts or aerial lifts. The single chair is a real relic of the past, and there are few still operating today. A double chair lift is common, and in many areas, triples and quadruples are in place.

For starters, always choose a beginner's lift. Virtually every area has one or two. The slopes are designed for learners and the lift runs slowly, making boarding and unloading easy. Some ski areas even have chair lifts specifically designed for kids.

Always get instructions if you are not familiar with the lift you're going to board. You and Roger should stand by and watch others load for a while.

Keep up the encouraging chatter. Talking and gently touching Roger on the shoulder or knee will make him feel secure while riding.

Never—*under any circumstances*—send a small child up a chair lift alone or with another small child. Always make sure a responsible adult is riding with Roger.

Problems getting off chair lifts are almost always caused by not being in the so-called "athletic position" (ankles, knees, and hips flexed, back rounded, head up, weight over the balls of the feet, and arms held comfortably in front of the body). You end up falling backward. How many times have you laughed at the sequence in every Warren Miller movie of the wet noodles getting off a chair lift? They are all falling backward. Be sure Roger remembers to be in a skiing position—knees bent, leaning forward. That way, it's easy.

Once Lindy was riding a double chair with Jessica, then age five. They'd done it a few times and both were fairly confident, so when Jessica said she'd like to get off without help, Lindy skied down the ramp.

Jessica never moved, and clearly it made for an interesting situation. The moral? Be sure they mean it and help send them on their way.

As you are ready to get up and go, place your hand behind Roger and help him push himself off. If kids are really small, you may have to lift them off for a while.

It's certainly possible for kids to learn to ski using aerial lifts, but the disadvantage is that the chance for earlier ski independence made possible by surface lifts is lost.

As long as Roger is having fun, the type of lift he rides is secondary. Only you and Roger can make it fun.

# YOUR SKIER'S CHECKLIST: CHAPTER SEVEN
## RIDING LIFTS

### SURFACE LIFTS

☐ Put skier between legs and step into tracks

☐ Be sure skis are parallel to lift cable

☐ Let go of handle (rope or T) and step to side

☐ Do not sit down when riding T-bar

☐ Grasp rope tow gently, then firmly

### CHAIR LIFTS

☐ Watch before loading and get instructions

☐ Be in athletic position for unloading

# EIGHT

# TURNING IN CONTROL— AGES THREE TO FIVE

*Please note: Timmy, age three, will be our guinea pig for this chapter. The next chapter deals with teaching six- to ten-year-olds to turn under control and we'll work with Jessica, age seven, at that point.*

*You may wish to read both chapters or simply read the one that applies to your child's age group. Some things are similar but many are different.*

Skiing isn't riding chair lifts and climbing up hills; it's skiing downhill. That's what we're going to talk about here.

First of all, keep offering encouragement.

"Look at you skiing down the hill! Isn't this wonderful? Look at you—you're a skier!"

Common sense is another ingredient that's important. Choose your hill carefully, and be sure that the slope you plan to work with is gentle and not very long. Even with Timmy held firmly in your grasp, you must teach him on a gentle hill.

Timmy will learn the feel of slow speeds he can control when he starts to ski on his own. You'll discover the value of a short hill soon enough when Timmy discovers he has to go to the bathroom.

What do we do with the ski poles? *Leave them at the bottom.* They simply get in the way.

The first time parent and child ski down the hill together at the Cochran Ski Area, we have you holding Timmy between your legs. He feels secure and you are in control. You can see and feel what he's doing.

Put Timmy between your legs at the top of the slope and hold him firmly at his waist. This puts you in control, while allowing him to ski. You can feel exactly what he's doing while he feels like he's skiing.

**The 3-5 year old needs close physical contact to begin turning. Start by skiing with him between your legs.**

Explain to him what's going to happen before you take off. Emphasize that you're not holding him up and that he needs to stand up on his own. Tell Timmy to bend his knees and then put his hands on his knees, so he has a balanced position.

He'll forget all this on the way down, of course, but if you continually encourage him and remind him, he'll eventually remember without your having to tell him.

Skiing, like so many sports, is done in what's called an athletic position. (We alluded to it in chapter 7 when talking about how

Be sure to teach
the athletic position.

to get off a chair lift.) The ankles, knees, and hips are flexed, with
weight over the balls of the feet and arms held comfortably in
front. The back is rounded, the head is up and alert, and the athlete
is ready to react.

So you can understand what Timmy is going through, you might
want to practice the position a bit at home, inside. Stand with your
feet about six inches apart. Flex your knees, drop your hips back,
and tilt forward at the waist. Hold your hands comfortably in front.
Experiment with your front and back balance. Lean forward and
feel the weight on your toes.

Tilt back and feel the weight under your heels. Put your hands
on your knees. Relax and notice where you feel your weight. It
should be under the balls of your feet back to the beginning of
your heels.

This position provides plenty of stability for both you and
Timmy. Front and back balance are critical. If your weight is too
far forward, the tails of your skis will be light and will skid. If
your weight is too far back, the tips of your skis will be light and
you will have difficulty in starting your turn.

Once Timmy learns to ski by himself, you might notice that
he skis with straight legs and bends at the waist. Children often
go through this stage. Don't worry about it.

Sometimes they'll become wet noodles.

He needs to develop the strength and flexibility in his legs to hold the athletic position and that will come in time. But when you're skiing down with Timmy, he needs to bend his legs so he won't throw you off.

OK, we're at the top of the hill and Timmy is between your legs. Using a snowplow, slowly ski back and forth across the hill.

"That's the way to keep your hands on your knees! Isn't this fun?" Keep encouraging him.

Two mistakes are common on the trip down the hill. Timmy will tend to relax and might slowly sink so that you're holding him up. Secondly, you may tend to take over and support him. In either instance, suggest to Timmy (and yourself) that he must support his own weight.

Feel him sagging? Here's what to say:

"Remember to stand on your skis. I'm not going to hold you up. Stand up and put your hands on your knees."

If he's still sagging, *bouncing* can often correct the problem. Still grasping Timmy by the waist, pick him up lightly, just enough to take the weight off his skis. Bounce him. He will usually resist and stand back up on his skis.

After you and Timmy have worked together for a while, you'll both feel comfortable. As you both gain confidence and begin to relax, you can release some of your support. Usually this is possible within a few hours.

There are several steps in relinquishing support. Begin by loosening your grip around Timmy's waist. It may be imperceptible to him, but you'll know you are taking the plunge into his skiing independence. Next, place your hands on top of his shoulders. Although you can still grip him firmly, this allows for much more freedom of movement. Maintain control by skiing slowly in a snowplow back and forth across the hill.

**It's time to relinquish support. Begin by loosening your grip around his waist.**

Place your hands on top of his shoulders.

After he gains confidence with these first techniques, grab the back of Timmy's jacket. Use one hand and be sure to grip it firmly. Again ski slowly in a snowplow back and forth. Losing him? Go back to the waist hold until you're ready to try again.

After he gains confidence, grab the back of his jacket.

By this time, Timmy should be ready to ski by himself. Look for a flat, gradual slope toward the bottom of the hill to let him fly on his own.

The run can be anywhere from two to twenty feet, but he should be able to glide to the bottom. Make sure the slope is so slight that Timmy will come to a natural stop by running out of speed.

Be sure and let him in on your thinking. Tell him you're going to let him ski on his own. Remind him to stand on his skis and to put his hands on his knees. When he seems to have his balance and is set, let him go!

It will be the same thrill you had when you saw him walk for the first time, but this time he's skiing. He'll be thrilled, too.

"You skied all by yourself! Look how far you went! Wasn't that fun? I'm proud of you!"

**Now he's skiing all by himself.**

## PLAY SOME NEW GAMES

Now it's game time again.

Try bump runs. Kids love to ski over bumps. Whenever a kid gets frustrated or otherwise out of sorts at the Cochran Ski Area, we take him on a bump run. Find a little bump over which you can ski. Ski slowly up the bump, schuss down the back side, and lift Timmy in the air at the end of the bump, talking all the way.

"Let's go find a bump we can ski over! Look—here's one! Here we go up, up, up. Down we go!"

Once Timmy's skied a bump run, he'll look for them every run.

Bird flight is another good game to play. Pretend you and Timmy are birds soaring through the air, banking first in one direction and then in another.

You'll develop a rhythm of dancing from your outside ski to outside ski as you bank to the outside of the turn.

When you are working with Timmy, try to avoid a mistake parents often make. You may both be leaning into the hill. It's easy and many skiers tend to do it. *Learn to lean away from the hill.* It's not natural, but it's the right way to do it. In a car, for example, we lean into the turn, but not in skiing. In order for our skis to hold, the weight has to come off the uphill (inside) ski and onto the downhill (outside) ski.

**Lean to the outside like a bird in flight.**

**Practice forming a V on the flats.**

This is done by lateral balance or side-to-side balance. The upper body leans to the outside (almost like a side bend) as your knees drive into the hill. When done properly, you should feel as if you could balance on your outside ski and actually pick up your inside ski.

Now you're ready to teach Timmy the very first step in learning to turn. The snowplow is the basis for all turns and control.

While seeing Timmy glide down the hill in skillful form is truly a thrill, it's going to take him longer to conquer the snowplow than it will an older child. Offer constant encouragement and be patient.

When Jessica was two, she learned to transfer the weight from one ski to the other, making basically parallel turns. She was indeed adorable to watch, schussing down the slope, but she had no control whatsoever. Once she discovered the braking power of the snowplow, we could venture anywhere together.

The snowplow, as we explained when we were working with older kids, is awkward for you and for Timmy.

Stand on the floor. Point your toes in while you push your heels out. Imagine having boots and skis attached to your feet as you slide down a hill. Expect Timmy to become frustrated at some point. It's only natural.

Pushing out knees while learning to
snowplow is a common mistake.

To introduce him to the snowplow, have him practice it on a
flat area at the bottom of the hill. Have him form a V or a triangle
with his skis. You may have to physically push the tails out by
tilting the skis on the inside edge and pushing out on the insides
of the boots. Having the ski on the inside edge is important for
control because this makes the skis plow against the snow.

Once Timmy has practiced the snowplow at the bottom, head
up the hill. Stay on the same gentle slope you've been working
on. At any sign of progress— however small it may be—greet it
with enthusiasm.

"Look at your V! Great job, Timmy. Can you make it bigger?
Great!"

If Timmy begins to push his knees out while learning the
snowplow—and that's a common mistake—have him try to touch
his knees together while pushing his heels and tails out. (A ski
on the outside edge prevents the skis from sliding easily into a
V position, and a flat ski doesn't offer enough resistance.)

## USE YOUR OWN SKIING ABILITY

Here's where your own skiing ability comes into play. There are basically three ways to accomplish teaching turns to Timmy.

With Timmy between your legs, hold onto him at the waist and have him form a V just like yours. Remind him to keep the tips in, while pushing the tails out. When you get near the bottom, let him try it on his own. As he gets more comfortable with the snowplow, have him go longer distances on his own.

Teach turns in control with child between your legs.

A different technique is to put your ski poles out to the side and have Timmy hang onto them. Both of you form a big snowplow and ski down the hill side by side. This gives Timmy a sense of freedom, yet you are still firmly in control.

Another technique for teaching turns keeps you in control: both of you hold a pole and ski downhill side by side.

The system we use at the Cochran Ski Area allows for more immediate feedback and corrections. Use the easier approaches unless you are quite confident of your own skiing ability.

Ski slowly backward in front of Timmy. Hold onto his ski tips and remind him to push out his tails. You may have to physcially push them out a few times until he gets the idea.

Some tots feel less secure with the adult in front, but you can

Ski slowly backward in front of Timmy, holding onto his tips.

show him you have complete control by letting him glide a short distance, stop him, and go again.

Each time you stop, say something like this:

"See, I can make you go and I can make you stop. I have complete control."

There are several advantages of this method. You have a ground-level visual view of the action and Timmy's progress. You can immediately correct things by holding his skis together and pushing his tails out, and you can offer him some freedom.

The disadvantages are that not all parents can handle skiing backward with much dexterity or skill, and since you have to take responsibility to stay out of other skiers' way, there could be a safety hazard if you aren't skilled at it.

Whatever method you choose, this skill will generally take Timmy quite awhile to learn. Be patient.

Once Timmy is pushing his tails out, he's ready to learn how to brake the snowplow. Now comes control.

**Skier coming down the hill in the snowplow position.**

As he comes down the hill in his snowplow, have him pull his skis together. Then have him quickly push his tails back into the V again. He will go faster as his skis come together. He'll slow down as soon as he's back into a snowplow. This is an initial taste of control.

Have Timmy experiment with the width of the V. Let him learn that the wider he makes it, the slower he'll go and the narrower he makes it, the faster he'll go.

Trust us—the following will happen:

You'll tell Timmy to push out his tails and he'll say, "I am! I am!"

It takes plenty of encouragement to get tots to really push out their tails. Try words like these:

"Let's see how big a V you can make. Can you make it bigger? Whew! Look at the big V you made. Did you feel how that slowed you down? Push your tails out again. Great!"

Conquering the braking snowplow is a major step toward the final goal of skiing down the hill in complete control.

The skier pulls his skis together.

The skier quickly pushes the ski tails back into the V.

## THE SNOWPLOW TURN

It's time to teach Timmy the snowplow turn. But first we need to remind him how to fall. There's the possibility now that he can get away from you, so be sure he understands that if you yell for him to fall, then he *must* fall.

Hold Timmy between your legs. Since he's more comfortable on skis now, just grab the back of his jacket. This allows more distance between you and Timmy and he has a sense of independence.

**When teaching snowplow turns, hold the back of the jacket.**

You can also use any of the other methods we described, such as poles to the side or your skiing backward. Again, the backward method is the best if you can handle it.

As the two of you move down the hill in your snowplow, have Timmy push out the tail of the ski opposite the direction of the turn.

This may sound confusing, but it's actually easy to follow. If Timmy is going to be turning left, he should push out the tail of the right ski. Turning right? Push out the left ski.

Push out the right ski to turn left.

Push out the left ski to turn right.

Once Timmy has a sense of how to turn, give him verbal cues. Pick out a couple of landmarks on opposite sides of the trail. Maybe it's the chair lift on one side or a big tree on the other.

Here's another fun way to learn which way to turn. Give Timmy two different colored mittens. Tell him to turn toward the blue mitten and then toward the red.

When he starts going too fast, don't hesitate to tell him to fall. Before long he should be able to ski by himself down an easy beginner's slope. And you're in for a thrill.

## SPECIAL DEVICES

We recommend teaching Timmy without using teaching aids, but they do exist and many parents find them helpful. They provide extra security and give you extra help.

The rope harness can be as simple as a rope tied around Timmy's waist with a long tail for you to hold onto, or it can be as sophisticated as a real canvass harness made especially for the purpose.

The harness works well for kids who can't quite manage to stay balanced without worrying about what — or who — is in front of them. If you feel more secure with a harness, go ahead and use one.

A word of caution: *take it completely off before loading any lift*.

Tip holders are devices designed to hold Timmy's tips together. When he's learning the snowplow, he can concentrate solely on pushing out his tails.

We prefer to hold the tips ourselves so that we can let go when ready. But if you are uncomfortable skiing backward and Timmy can't get his tips together, try them. Just use the tip holders long enough for him to get the idea, however.

Special devices won't be easy to find (try a full service ski shop first). Innovation may be necessary.

Using poles to the side is a teaching method we described earlier. It offers some freedom, plus it maintains control for you.

Don't use poles in the front. We've seen this approach used and there are too many disadvantages.

When the poles are held comfortably for you, they are too high for Timmy. When they're right for him, you have to bend too far down. It just doesn't work.

To emphasize turning skills, there are several games to play. Start with follow the leader. Have Timmy follow you down the hill as you go over bumps and around obstacles. Switch and have Timmy lead. He'll love being able to guide you around the hill. What a sense of accomplishment!

Try playing train. This is really just an extension of follow the leader. The leader becomes the engine who enlists other skiers to become the cars and a final person to be the caboose. This game is really fun for accomplished ski tots.

The wrong way to do it: poles in front are too high for the child.

Poles in front are too low for the parent.

Play the airplane game.

Airplane works well now. Have Timmy extend his arms straight out to the side. When he turns, have him bend his waist toward the downhill ski (that's the ski opposite the turn, remember). Continue it down the hill, pretending he's an airplane. Add sound effects for fun.

Slalom is another fun game, and you can also do this with other skiers. Set poles down a hill as turning cues. Make sure they are far enough apart so they are easy to go around. Try doing the airplane around the poles; this is a good way to get the weight on the downhill ski. The arm nearest the pole should be up.

Picking daisies is similar to airplane. Have Timmy reach down toward the outside of the downhill ski boot to pick an imaginary daisy.

**Touch the boot when playing the daisy game.**

Have him alternate picking daisies from one downhill boot to the other as he moves down the hill. Be sure he bends *sideways* at the waist so all the weight of the upper body goes out over the downhill ski, not just the hand.

Jeannie was a ski tot we worked with who defied the system. Instead of leaning over by putting weight on the downhill ski to pick the daisy, she reached straight down to the boot, not making any turns at all. But she did touch her boots and picked plenty of daisies.

Now that Timmy has made some real progress by learning how to fall, snowplow, and turn in control, he can gradually take on more difficult terrain. Before heading down a new slope, however, be sure and rehearse how to fall the right way—into the hill.

For steeper terrain, your child can learn to traverse and turn. First comes a long traverse. . .

. . .continue the turn across the hill. . .

. . .still continue the turn across the hill.

Timmy now has two ways to control his speed. The length of the turn is one way. On steeper terrain, he can turn longer, going across the hill (called a traverse). The wider he makes his snowplow, the more he can control his speed.

Yet, the wide snowplow is only effective up to a point. Beyond that, it becomes too wide and Timmy plops on his backside. The long traverse is more effective on steeper terrain.

To make the point, take Timmy on a trail with some varying terrain so that as you ski down the hill the trail gets steeper, flatter, then steeper.

Tell Timmy that when you get to the steeper parts of the trail, you want him to go back and forth from one side to the other following you. If he gets going too fast, or gets in front of you, tell him to fall.

When you get into the flatter section of the slope, continue the long traverse until you come to a stop. Explain to Timmy that as he comes off a steeper section, he can make shorter turns.

For comparison purposes, ski long traverses on the steeper sections and shorten them on the flatter sections. Do that a few times for emphasis. Once he's conquered this step, the whole mountain is his!

Now what? Ski, that's what. Ski, ski, ski.

Timmy doesn't need any more advanced instruction at this point. He's officially a skier! Ski often and have fun doing it!

Tots can go too fast on steeper terrain with short traverses.

A short traverse means quick turns down the hill.

A narrow snowplow does not slow the tot down enough on steeper terrain.

The wider the snowplow, the better the control in the steeps.

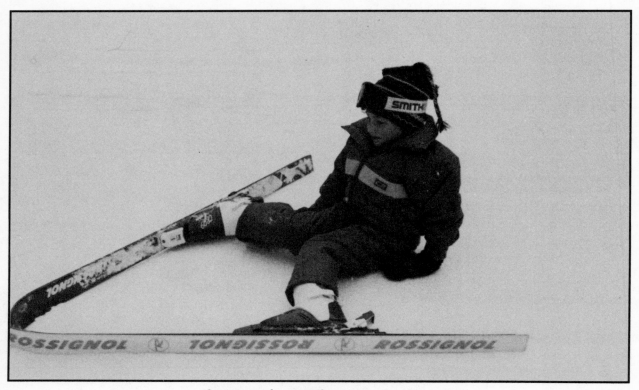

Sometimes the snowplow can get too big.

# YOUR SKIER'S CHECKLIST: CHAPTER EIGHT

### PARENT AND CHILD TOGETHER
- ☐ Hold child at waist
- ☐ Child supports own weight
- ☐ Child bends knees
- ☐ Child's hands are on knees
- ☐ Child can ski by himself from two to twenty yards

### GAMES TO PLAY
- ☐ Bump run
- ☐ Bird flight

### SNOWPLOW WITHOUT TURNS
- ☐ Practice V on flat
- ☐ Practice V coming downhill
  - ☐ Between your legs
  - ☐ Poles to side
  - ☐ You ski backward

### BRAKING SNOWPLOW
- ☐ Push tails out, pull tails together

### SNOWPLOW TURNS
- ☐ Child skis downhill, you remain in control
- ☐ Child pushes out tail of ski opposite direction of turns
- ☐ Child turns to verbal cues

### MORE GAMES TO PLAY
- ☐ Follow the leader
- ☐ The train
- ☐ The airplane
- ☐ Slalom
- ☐ Picking daisies

### BEYOND THE SNOWPLOW
- ☐ Longer turns (traverses) for steeper terrain
- ☐ Wider snowplow for steeper terrain
- ☐ Ski!
- ☐ Ski!
- ☐ Ski!
- ☐ Ski some more!

# TURNING IN CONTROL— AGES SIX TO TEN

The day Jessica was learning to turn and got away from Lindy's husband, Steve, he experienced that awful wrenching feeling in the pit of his stomach we've all come to know at one time or another.

Steve watched in fear as she skied straight toward a snowmobile. He desperately reached for her as she hooked a tip and flipped head over heels. She was shaken from a bad fall but the result was only a fat lip.

Amy headed straight for the Mitey Mite lift on another day. Bobby felt the same way as Steve when he watched Amy topple over. She was no more seriously hurt than Jessica.

The point is turning helps kids—and all of us—ski in control. That's why this chapter and what you do about it are so vitally important.

Mastering turning extends our world. It offers control and that, in turn, allows us to ride lifts, enjoy longer trails, and handle more difficult terrain. Knowing that your own Jessica and Amy are skiing under control makes the sport enjoyable for *you*, too.

Tom will be our superstar in this learning experience for children six to ten years old. And, as always, just substitute your own child's name when you read it and imagine him or her in Tom's boots.

Tom will progress very quickly (within hours or at worst a day or two) to the snowplow turn, but it can take years to get to the parallel for many children. Some—particularly six- and seven-year-olds—may not be interested in anything beyond the snowplow.

Don't worry about parallel turns. Once Tom can turn, let him ski. Eight- to ten-year-olds will show more interest in learning to ski parallel, but all kids are different. They'll let you know when they're ready for it.

Lindy was nearly seven when she became determined to ski parallel. One day she ran into the lodge at Smuggler's Notch and told Mom and Dad, "I can ski parallel!"

Out came the camera while Lindy demonstrated. She skied across the hill, did a snowplow turn, teeter-tottered back and forth as she attempted to lift her uphill ski to set it parallel to her other ski, and grinned from ear to ear for the camera.

Barbara Ann liked the snowplow's security. Even when she made the U.S. Ski Team at age fifteen, she was still really in the snowplow position. She was simply transferring weight from one ski to the other, so her skis carved. Her technique was both efficient and fast, but it certainly confused her coaches, who nicknamed her "Scooter." It wasn't until a coach at a training camp in Chile told her to keep her knees together that she actually skied parallel.

## SKIING IN CONTROL

Before we work on the snowplow turn for Tom, review what we've learned about skiing in control. Push his skis in a wide V to slow down and stop. (Remember, at this age, poles are optional. If he wants them, use them. When he gets into parallel skiing, he will need them for timing.)

Practice falling into the hill again. Tom has to be able to control his speed *at all times*.

Look for a practice hill that is perhaps three times the length he's been climbing. With a gentle slope, he'll be able to control his speed.

A skier must put the ski *on edge* and then apply pressure so it will bend in an arc. Since the skis are already on edge in the snowplow, all that is necessary now is the pressure.

The simplest way to get to the pressure point is to ask Tom to push one ski out more than the other, while still maintaining the V position. To turn right, out goes the left ski. To turn left, the right one goes out more.

Encourage Tom to slow down to a stop before he shifts his skis into the fall line (the line a snowball would follow down the hill). By beginning the turn without speed, he won't feel out of control as his skis pick up speed into the fall line. He can concentrate on pushing his ski out wide and coming around to complete the turn. This is a nice confidence builder.

If you don't use this method, Tom will no doubt pick up speed, feel out of control, perhaps panic, and head straight downhill. He'll forget all he's learned and will fall straight back on the skis.

Put the ski on edge, apply pressure, and the ski bends in an arc.

One technique for teaching is to ski directly in front of him, with Tom right behind. If he gets in a jam, he can ski right into you and you can control his speed. Then just separate and try it again.

Parent has the child follow right behind.

## STRONG SKIERS CAN GO
## BACKWARD TO HELP

If you are a strong skier as we described in Chapter 8, skiing backward in front of Tom can be very effective. It's not easy on you, however, as you must keep looking downhill to see what—or who—is behind you. Essentially you are in a backward snowplow position. Your *tails* are together and your *tips* are apart as you face *uphill*.

Now you can hold Tom's tips together while he pushes his tails out. Continually remind him that he can *always stop* by falling into the hill. Now it's time for some games that reinforce learning.

Start with follow the leader and lead Tom back and forth across the hill. As he masters turning, make this game interesting by skiing over bumps and varying the turns. Do long turns and then quick changes in direction. Allow Tom to lead for variety. He'll love it.

Play airplane, too. Pretend you and Tom are airplanes gliding through the friendly skies. Ski in a snowplow, but put both arms straight out to the side. Tip your wings (arms) to the outside of each turn, as if you're banking in an airplane. This game is great for six- to eight-year-olds, but once they hit nine and ten, it could be considered baby stuff.

Way back in the beginning of our book we began to sing the praises of carving turns. When it comes to learning the wedge turn, our next subject, carving is the perfect means for control.

At the Cochran Ski Area we believe in teaching skiers to carve. It enables you to ski more difficult terrain, and you will always be in control.

Carving simply means that the ski turns on an arc. If you were to put a dot on the snow and passed *through* that dot while turning, your entire ski would pass over that dot. Too many skiers skid through their turns, meaning that their skis slide sideways.

Compare skidding and carving to driving an automobile. When you skid through a turn in a car, you may not have lost control, but you certainly don't have as much control as you do when your tires hug the road and pull your car through the turn.

The same thing applies to skiing. You probably won't lose control by skidding through a turn, but you are not going to be in as much control as when you've been carving.

## WEDGE TURNS ARE DIFFERENT
## THAN SNOWPLOWS

That brings us to the wedge turn. The only significant difference between the wedge turn and a snowplow is in the distribution of weight. The wedge turn maintains the snowplow position but transfers the weight completely from both skis, in the snowplow position, to outside ski to outside ski. The ski *slides* in a snowplow; it *carves* in a wedge.

Tom should lean to the outside now with his upper body. He should feel like he's doing a side bend. When he wants to turn right, he must lean to his *left*.

When the weight is transferred correctly in the wedge, Tom can feel his skis react. He needs to remember—and you need to remind him—that his skis need to be up on edge (snowplow position) to be able to carve and also bent in an arc by exerting pressure on the outside ski. Then the ski will perform.

Skiers often make a very common mistake by leaning into the hill. *Tom must lean away from the hill to have more control and to turn easily.* Skiing is indeed different from most everything else we do and, when done properly, we should feel as if we could balance on our outside ski and actually pick up our inside ski.

One way to be absolutely sure that Tom is weighting only the inside ski is to tell him to get all his weight off his uphill ski. If he can lift the inside ski throughout the turn, his weight is definitely on his outside ski.

**Practice leaning to the outside on slalom course.**

## MORE GAMES TO PLAY

Let's play some more games now to practice.

Slalom course is played by setting up a series of five to ten objects from ski poles to road cones. Have Tom turn around the objects, practicing leaning to the outside of the turn (away from the pole or cone).

Try a tilted pole course by setting up a set of five to ten turns like you did with the slalom course, except this time tilt each pole so Tom has to lean away from the turn.

The most fun game of all is the human slalom. You'll need a group of at least seven or eight people to play. The first one skis down a turn and sets himself like a pole.

The second person skis around the first human pole, skis down another turn, and sets himself in place. Everyone continues in this manner until the course is set.

Then the top person (Tom) skis the course and becomes the bottom pole, and the game continues until everyone has a chance to ski the course.

In the tilted pole course, the skier must lean away from the turn.

The stem christie is the next logical step to learn on the way to parallel skiing, and it's actually the beginning of the parallel turn.

The wedge turn is still used to complete the turn, but the skis are pulled together as the skier traverses across the hill. That's really what Lindy was demonstrating for the family cameras at age seven.

When Tom indicates a desire to ski parallel, the place to begin is with the stem christie. Demonstrate it first and then have Tom try it.

Start out by making a wedge turn. As you ski across the hill, let your skis run together until they are parallel.

**To start the wedge, weight should be on both skis.**

**Apply pressure to the outside ski.**

To make the next turn, push your skis back into the snowplow, slow down, lean to the outside with your upper body, and complete the wedge turn. As you traverse across the hill in the opposite direction, pull your skis together. Repeat the process and then have Tom do it.

Watch your expectations about the parallel turn. Tom will progress very quickly from a novice to an intermediate skier who has mastered the snowplow and wedge turns.

**Weight is completely on the downhill ski.**

**At the end of the carved turn, pull skis together.**

## IT TAKES TIME TO SKI PARALLEL

Now it's going to take plenty of time—as we said earlier—for him to become proficient at the parallel turn. Don't even begin teaching him until he is completely competent and confident with the wedge.

The parallel turn, however, is actually quite similar to the wedge turn. Weight is still transferred from outside ski to outside ski by leaning with the upper body. But there are several differences. The skis are parallel now, with the tips together and tails out, instead of in a V. The ski must be put on edge by driving the outside knee forward and into the hill. The skis are already on edge in the wedge. The front and back balance is more critical in a parallel turn, while in the wedge, the V provides a stable platform.

You might want to look back in chapter 8 and read where we suggest you practice that athletic position in your living room before trying to teach it.

When you are teaching Tom the parallel turn, tell him to ski with his skis together. Explain that he'll begin his turn just like he did in the wedge, by leaning to the outside of the turn with his upper body.

Then he must drive his outside knee forward and immediately into the hill to get his outside ski on edge. He must finish the turn to remain in control. By that we mean he must continue to weight the outside (downhill) ski and keep turning until he is almost turning back up the hill.

Skiing parallel does not mean keeping the skis and legs together. That's a common misconception. The knees must be slightly separate (about six inches) so the legs can function independently.

A skier must weight the outside ski by driving the knee into the hill (called angulating). We're only talking about the outside knee. When both knees are together, the skier will be forced to angulate both knees, which just forces weight back onto the inside ski.

As Tom improves, encourage him to put more pressure on his skis. By leaning to the outside, he is putting some pressure on the ski to bend it in an arc, but he can do quicker, harder turns by supplying more pressure with the strength in his legs.

Have Tom imagine he is trying to jump as high as he can to touch a ceiling. What would he do? He'd drop down low and then explode to push off the floor and jump as high as he can. He does the same thing in skiing, except he doesn't allow himself to come up until he has completed the turn. He should imagine that he's trying to push the length of the ski a half a foot under the snow.

Skis should be parallel but about six inches apart.

Drive the downhill knee into the hill to weight the outside ski.

Next comes the pole plant. It's not necessary in skiing, but it makes parallel turning easier by initiating the turn and providing a point around which to turn.

As Tom anticipates the start of a new turn, he should bring his downhill arm up and open his wrist to face downhill. The hand and pole will be cocked at an angle. This movement provides a sense of timing to begin his next turn.

Next, he should jab his pole quickly into the snow, but he doesn't leave it there. The jab simply gives him a spot around which to turn, rather than turning around the pole itself.

Tom's a hot skier now. So just let him ski to his heart's content!

To plant the pole, bring the downhill arm up, open the wrist, and jab the pole quickly into the snow.

# YOUR SKIER'S CHECKLIST: CHAPTER NINE

### PARENT AND CHILD TOGETHER

☐ Ski with child close behind you

☐ Ski backward watching downhill

### SNOWPLOW TURN

☐ Push one ski out, then the other, maintaining V

☐ Stop before shifting ski into fall line

☐ Remind child to fall into the hill

### GAMES TO PLAY

☐ Follow the leader

☐ Airplane

### THE WEDGE TURN

☐ Weight is transferred from outside ski to outside ski

☐ Ski carves, not slides

☐ Skier leans away from hill

### MORE GAMES TO PLAY

☐ Slalom course

☐ Tilted pole course

☐ Human slalom

### STEM CHRISTIE

☐ Wedge is used to complete turn

☐ Skis are pulled together during traverse

☐ Push back to snowplow for next turn

### PARALLEL TURNS

☐ Temper your expectations

☐ Weight transfers from outside ski to outside ski

☐ Put ski on edge by driving outside knee forward into hill

## TEN

# SO MANY DIFFERENT PERSONALITIES

When photographer "Snowflake" Bentley showed us each and every snowflake was different, he made a point that is very important to us as we teach our children to ski. Each child is different and each has his or her distinct personality.

Some children are independent and determined. They are willing to try what we suggest and many things that we don't. They have no fear of making mistakes.

Others have the feeling that someone will always be there to protect them. There's not a fear of getting hurt because someone will be there to catch them if they fall.

Still others are timid. They believe they can't do anything successfully, so why try?

Some sag. Some are stiff. Some know everything. Some won't listen.

There are kids who take two runs and quit, while others cling to their parents. Some won't dare ride a lift.

We've had experience with all of the above and more. We'll describe them for you and offer some ways to work with them.

Start with independence and it comes right down to Lindy's daughter, Jessica, for the perfect example.

Jessica is determined to succeed and will try anything to get to that point. She could care less if she makes a mistake along the way. Making mistakes helps her learn.

Working with a Jessica can be very rewarding because of her sheer determination. The danger comes with the fact that she's seldom aware of the risks involved. When you are working with her, you must allow for the independence yet remain alert and ready to help.

She took to skiing at age one. She would go get her boots and struggle to put them on. She learned to walk around on her skis and sometimes would head down a slope. We let her go but were always ready when she got into that inevitable trouble.

By two, she wanted to ride the Mitey Mite. Her desire was fueled when Roger, her cousin (ten months her senior), mastered it. She walked to the lift, grabbed on, rode about twenty feet, and fell forward, banging her forehead on the snow.

Marilyn went over to help, but Jessica began to scream. She wasn't upset because she was hurt, only that Marilyn was trying to help her. If Roger could ride that lift, she could, too!

Marilyn dropped back to the next handle and followed Jessica to the top. We couldn't let her wait too long at the top or she'd attempt to ski down by herself.

We've worked with children who have been too dependent, overly protected. They have relied on others to take care of their every need, and they often have no fear of getting hurt because they know adults wouldn't let that happen.

Working with a dependent child tries one's patience and requires lots of encouragement. It also requires forcing the child to take risks.

Jessica's friend Sam was learning to ski at age three, and he had no worries at all. He knew if he got going too fast, someone would catch him and stop him. He didn't worry about how fast he was going or how he would stop. Someone always protected him.

One day we took Sam skiing. He had tremendous balance and no fear. We took him to the top of the T-bar, and as we started gliding across the hill he headed straight for the woods. He had no idea he was in any danger and was looking back talking to Jessica.

Barbara Ann caught up to him before he struck a tree.

On the way down, we took turns skiing with him between our legs. When the slope was gradual, we let him go by himself. We showed him how to fall and explained that when we yelled "Fall!" he should plop down on that imaginary dot on his hip.

Time after time he'd head down the hill and we'd yell "Fall!" and he'd pick up speed and stand on his skis. We'd reprimand him for not falling, but he didn't care.

Finally, we decided to take him down to the beginner slope and let him ski out of control. We explained we were *not* going to stop him. If he wanted to stop, he would have to fall and that was all there was to it.

Sam really didn't believe that we wouldn't stop him. We yelled "Fall!" as usual and he paid no attention. When he was going faster than he ever had gone before, he finally realized we weren't going to grab him, so he fell. He was scared and furious with us.

We refused to pick him up, insisting that he try his best. We weren't sure what made him madder: the fact that we let him fall or that we didn't pick him up immediately.

Shortly after this experience, Sam learned to ski and became responsible for his own actions.

## THE I-CAN'T-DO-IT KID

Robert will be our "I-can't-do-it" child. This is one of the most frustrating personalities to teach how to ski.

Robert believes he can't do anything successfully. Some children who believe they can't are quite content in manipulating others to do tasks for them. Still others refuse to do anything at all. The most difficult of this breed whine or cry while they install themselves on their rear ends at the bottom of the hill.

Perseverance and consequences are required with Roberts. One such skier we met maneuvered others into buckling his boots, putting his skis on for him, and pushing him up the hill so he didn't have to sidestep. He sure loved skiing. Why not?

We insisted that Robert must *try* to buckle his boots himself, that he *try* to put his own skis on, and that he *try* to sidestep up the hill.

If he made a good, honest effort and then needed some help, we gave it to him. He learned as much as he could, while we offered as little aid as possible.

We generally tell kids who refuse to attempt anything they are told to try, "It's not that you *can't* do this, it's that you *won't* do it." That's a big difference. We explain that the way you learn is by making mistakes and you have to try and do your best.

Children like Robert who cry and whine while refusing to do anything need to be given consequences. For example, tell them if they are going to cry, you are not going to instruct them. You don't have to work with them if they are whining or crying. You also don't have to listen to them. If they want to learn how to ski, they'll have to listen to you and put a smile on their face.

You might try the Tom Sawyer technique. In plain sight of Robert, play games with other children or ski down by yourself, having a wonderful time. Ignore the crying child until he stops.

## THE SCARECROW CHILD

The "scarecrow" child just sags so much you wonder if she has a muscle in her body. Poor muscle control and lack of strength contribute to this personality type.

These children require more help at first. As they begin to master skills, however, their muscle tone improves. Skiing exercises these muscles and makes them stronger.

One little girl we worked with was born with a birth defect

that damaged some nerves and the muscles in her legs. She can walk, but her legs are weak.

She was three years old the first time we took her skiing. She didn't have the strength in her legs to lift her skis to sidestep, but she could shuffle her skis along.

On the second outing, she was able to lift her skis. As she skied between our legs, we would often feel her sink until we were holding her up. We constantly reminded her to stand on her own. Sometimes bouncing her would help, other times we'd let her continue sinking until she realized she had to stand or she'd sit on her tails.

She still requires plenty of help, but she is able to walk on a gentle slope and glide on her own. Her muscle tone improves with the exercise.

## THE TIN MAN

The "tin man"—Georgie—is the opposite of the scarecrow child. He's stiff, either because he's not very flexible or because he's petrified of skiing.

If flexibility is the problem, try some warm-up exercises. Reach for the sky by putting both arms overhead and reaching as high as you can. Or with your arms overhead, tilt to the side, doing a side bend. Do it to the right and to the left. Try touching your boot tops or ski tips by gradually bending forward from the waist.

Encourage Georgie to get into the position you want and if he's having a difficult time, gently move him into position. Encourage, but don't force.

Most children are flexible. Generally we become more rigid as we grow older. Stiffness usually is associated with fear. Constantly reassure Georgie that you have control. Be sure his hands are on his knees and that he goes slowly. Once he realizes he won't get hurt, he'll begin to relax.

The "tin man" needs exercises to become more flexible.

First, reach for the sky and stretch.

The sidebend stretch should be done to the left and to the right.

Try to touch the tips of your skis for a real stretch.

# THE KNOW-IT-ALL

The "know-it-all" won't listen. Why should he, since he already has all the answers. He'll finish sentences for you and after you tell him something, he'll mutter, "I know!"

Barbara Ann was a hostess for *Sports Illustrated* advertisers at the Lake Placid Olympic Games in 1980 and encountered an adult version of the know-it-all she'll never forget.

John insisted that he'd enjoy skiing the Whiteface Mountain downhill course because speed gave him such a thrill. He had never before been on skis but knew the experience would be similar to racing motorcycles, which was his hobby.

Barbara Ann finally convinced him to go on an outing to a nearby ski area that offered beginner and intermediate terrain.

He refused lessons because "skiing wasn't hard." Barbara Ann let him ride the T-bar, admonishing him to get off halfway.

Barely able to get off the T-bar, he struggled to shuffle his skis along a flat path to get to the slope. After about ten feet, he fell. He couldn't get up. Soon he realized he wasn't so smart. Eventually John decided skiing wasn't for him.

If you have a know-it-all child, you will have to set the guidelines. Insist that he listen to you and have him repeat the instructions. If he attempts to do something you feel he's not ready for, only let him attempt it if there is reason to believe he won't hurt himself by trying it. When you've proved your point, insist he follow your instructions to be allowed to continue skiing.

"Two-Run" Sally is another interesting case. Some tots endure two runs and then insist it's time to go back inside for hot chocolate. Since her attention span is limited, keep her happy. Take her in for a while, but bring her back out again. You'll need lots of patience, but it will eventually pay off. Gradually, Sally will stay out for longer and longer spells.

"Clinging" Claudia won't let go of your leg. You need to talk to her firmly, but gently. Reassure her that you have complete control.

Place her hands on her knees. Go forward and stop. Say something like this: "See! I can stop and go. I won't let you go!"

There are as many different personalities among skiing kids as there are snowflakes. Try to understand them. The payoff will come sooner than you expect.

## ELEVEN
# RACING: IT GETS IN YOUR BLOOD

It was just ten minutes before the start of the slalom in the Olympic Games in Sapporo, Japan. The rep checked my bindings. The coach spread wax on my skis. I pumped my legs up and down to get the blood flowing. Seven minutes. . . .

I unzipped my warm-ups and handed them to the coach. The wind whipped the snow into my face and chilled my muscles. I slid into the tent. Four minutes. . . .

The first forerunners stepped into the starting gate. The coach rubbed my legs. I tried to relax. Three minutes. . . .

I pulled off my parka and I was left alone. One minute.

I planted my poles. Ten seconds. . . .

Three deep breaths. Beep, beep, beep, beep, beep, BEEP!

*From a college composition*
*by Olympic Gold Medalist*
*Barbara Ann Cochran*

It would be ludicrous, wouldn't it, for us to end our book on teaching your kids to ski without discussing racing and the thrills it provides?

Once your skier—we'll call him Doug this time— shows an interest in racing, give him the chance to try it before you begin to spend lots of money to outfit him and set him up on a racing team.

Some ski areas offer fun races or club racing programs for free or for a nominal fee.

The Lollipop races at the Cochran Ski Area are held every Sunday afternoon. There's no charge, and every entrant receives a lollipop for competing. The local paper even carries the best times of the day.

Ski areas run National Standard races (NASTAR) where a fee is paid for every run made. You compete for a time and are given a handicap based on age and sex. Your time is compared against a pacesetter's time. You may win a gold, silver, or bronze medal by finishing within a certain time of the pacesetter. NASTAR has developed a program for children that is exciting and it offers good race training.

If Doug is interested in racing, encourage him to join a club and compete in local races or, perhaps, in a Buddy Werner League. (Werner was an Olympic racer from Steamboat Springs, Colorado, who was killed in an avalanche.)

These are organized races where Doug becomes a member of a ski team that has a coach. The main virtue is that he spends time practicing his skiing skills.

As Doug gets better at racing and develops his interest, he could join the United States Ski Association (USSA) and race in what are known as sanctioned events. There is a fee to join USSA, as well as a registration fee for every race.

## CONSIDER SEVERAL FACTORS

There are a number of things to consider when Doug gets involved with a racing program.

Always give him the opportunity without applying pressure. Let him know he can run in the fun races without forcing him to train and that he doesn't have to race every weekend. Encourage plenty of free skiing. Keep it fun.

He doesn't need fancy equipment to race, but keep the equipment he has well tuned. His edges should be sharp, bottoms in good repair, and waxed.

We overheard a parent at a race for kids thirteen years old and younger making the point to another parent that the kids "were having too much fun racing," implying they weren't working hard enough. Our way of thinking about ski racing is exactly the opposite. If it isn't fun for Doug, he shouldn't be doing it.

Provide him with an opportunity to train but without schedules. Don't tell him early on that he *has* to train. As he gets older and really wants to excel, he'll *want* to train.

Start off on easy hills. Even at the beginning of each new season, racers like to begin their training on milder hills. As confidence begins to build, they will graduate to more difficult terrain.

Be sure to keep Doug warm at the races. There's no reason to take off parkas and warm-ups at fun races. It's more important that he stays warm and has a good time.

Once he gets to higher levels, he may race in a ski suit or a sweater and ski pants. In either case, be sure he's warm until he's ready to start. Having someone at the top bring his parka to the bottom is important.

There are a number of considerations when choosing a ski club or racing program for Doug.

You'll want to be sure the ski area truly supports the program and it cares about providing a quality operation. Make sure the area will let kids run gates and has a race training area for kids and coaches. Is there a lift nearby to the training site?

Most good ski racing programs have facilities set aside for the activity. There's a timing building, ski tuning area, storage place for poles, timing equipment, and video recorders.

Be sure to add up everything the racing program will cost you, so you don't get surprised. Often there's a season pass you'll need to purchase and dues for coaching and racing.

But is it worth it? Sure it is—whether the prize is a trip to an Olympic victory stand or a lick on a lollipop.

Let's check back in on Barbara Ann's essay.

The gates slid past me. My mind was numb. Turn after turn, I had no thoughts except to get to the finish. I kept going and then I was through.

I had made it. I could have won, but I was too scared to look. I was stunned by silence. And, then Rick and Bobby yelled. I was surrounded by hugs and kisses. Then I knew. I had won a Gold Medal.

# YOUR SKIER'S CHECKLIST: CHAPTER ELEVEN

## ON BECOMING A RACER

- ☐ Join a club or local race program
- ☐ Compete in fun races
- ☐ Start off on easy hills and stay warm
- ☐ Graduate into USSA race programs, if still having fun
- ☐ Don't say "you *have* to train"
- ☐ Be sure ski area supports race program

# TWELVE

# THE FINISHING TOUCHES

There's a question that always seems to come up in family debates over dinner or whenever industry marketing types seem to need something to spark an earnest discussion: when does a person become a skier?

Is a skier someone who comes down a mountain twenty-four times or sixty-eight times? Is a skier someone who wears funny clothes and pink racing goggles? Is a skier someone whose little nose runs at all the wrong times? Is a skier someone who can't get a smile off his or her face when the turn is made just right? The answer, of course, is all of the above. Being a skier is something that is worn inside out.

We believe skiers are created with that first move that provides a true sense of accomplishment. When Jimmy finally slides one ski past the other, when Amy rides the Mitey Mite lift to the top "all by myself!" and when Tom has his boots buckled and is on the way to the chair lift at 8:00 A.M. before you get the car parked in the lot, that's when skiers are made.

We hope that you have helped nurture a new skier into the fold and that our book has made the process smoother. This sport has a way of keeping us interested for a lifetime.

So, what's next?

After some time on snow, so to speak, if you have maintained your patience and sanity, you are the proud parents of a good snowplower or wedge skier.

From this point on, the skiing, the fun, the exuberance, and the ability level of your skier will only get better. The pressure is off, the learning curve is on.

Take time at this plateau to enjoy skiing with Jimmy or Jessica, Roger or Amy—really enjoy it. Once again, you may be closing in on that fateful point in time when they'll pass you on the mountain for good.

Soon enough, you'll want to go on to the next steps. You'll want to help them begin the serious approach to parallel skiing and the expert levels. Then again, maybe you won't. We noted earlier in our book that some children are quite satisfied with the snowplow or wedge for long periods of time.

Eventually that will modify into a parallel profile or close to it, but if it never does and skiing remains fun and safe, then so be it.

We are a family of ski racers and love the thrill of competition. And our parents used racing as a means to teach us about life and the lessons it held for us. But had we not taken so readily to the racecourse, we would no doubt have been just as enthusiastic to be free-skiing our way to adulthood.

Your attitude toward skiing becomes very important now. Don't become a fair-weather skier waiting for blue skies and fluffy snow. Go skiing when you and Timmy want to go, not when the weather forecast says the conditions will be ideal. Ski often; that's how lifetime sports really develop.

Reinforcement is important. Remember to praise Amy continually for that "perfect wedge turn" and to tell Tom that he really has learned to "ride that triple chair" just like you do.

Perhaps it's time to plan that family ski vacation. Go for it. You owe yourself that trip to Colorado or Utah, to Europe or New England.

We can't help but add this thought: the Cochran family has skied all over the world, yet, we taught our kids to ski here on our little hilltop in northern Vermont.

Take the trips and enjoy the wide world of skiing. But for everyday training, practice, fun, and—most important of all—memory making as a family, always come home. Every skier we know has his or her warmest thoughts for that place on earth where skis hit snow the very first time. Nurture that feeling.

Writers love to wax about that elusive ski experience. Yet, without ever defining it precisely, it is why we want our kids to become skiers, why they will bring their kids to our mountains as well. And, on it goes.